PERGAMON INTERNATIONAL LIBRARY
of Science, Technology, Engineering and Social Studies
The 1000-volume original paperback library in aid of education,
industrial training and the enjoyment of leisure
Publisher: Robert Maxwell, M.C.

ASPECTS OF MANAGEMENT

THE PERGAMON TEXTBOOK
INSPECTION COPY SERVICE

An inspection copy of any book published in the Pergamon International Library will
gladly be sent to academic staff without obligation for their consideration for course
adoption or recommendation. Copies may be retained for a period of 60 days from
receipt and returned if not suitable. When a particular title is adopted or recommended for
adoption for class use and the recommendation results in a sale of 12 or more copies, the
inspection copy may be retained with our compliments. The Publishers will be pleased to
receive suggestions for revised editions and new titles to be published in this important
International Library.

ASPECTS OF MANAGEMENT

by

SAMUEL EILON

Imperial College of Science and Technology, London

PERGAMON PRESS

OXFORD · NEW YORK · TORONTO · SYDNEY · PARIS · FRANKFURT

U.K.	Pergamon Press Ltd., Headington Hill Hall, Oxford OX3 0BW, England
U.S.A.	Pergamon Press Inc., Maxwell House, Fairview Park, Elmsford, New York 10523, U.S.A.
CANADA	Pergamon of Canada Ltd., 75 The East Mall, Toronto, Ontario, Canada
AUSTRALIA	Pergamon Press (Aust.) Pty. Ltd., 19a Boundary Street, Rushcutters Bay, N.S.W. 2011, Australia
FRANCE	Pergamon Press SARL, 24 rue des Ecoles, 75240 Paris, Cedex 05, France
WEST GERMANY	Pergamon Press GmbH, 6242 Kronberg-Taunus, Pferdstrasse 1, Frankfurt-am-Main, West Germany

First edition 1977

Library of Congress Catalog Card no. 76-47081

Printed in Great Britain by Biddles Ltd., Guildford, Surrey

0 08 020968 8 (Flexicover)
0 08 020969 6 (Hardcover)

CONTENTS

PREAMBLE

There are many issues on the management scene that demand our attention, from issues relating to the very ethos of the industrial enterprise—the justification and distribution of profits, the function of the board of directors, and the ramifications of worker participation—to issues associated with motivation of the individual and with styles of management. And then there are some fundamental problems in such areas as analysis of performance, corporate excellence, the possible contribution of operational research modelling to the decision-making process. What do we mean by research in the field of management, how scientific is the work of the management scientist, and what are his responsibilities in the industrial environment?

These are problems that managers and students of the management activity constantly encounter. There are problems of ethics, of methodology, of measurement, and of evaluation. The literature on management—and it is vast—abounds with answers, and the management gurus—and there are many—are ever ready with instant advice. That we often find contradictions in the literature and genuine disagreements is only to be expected, but we also find ambiguities, fashions, myths, and dogmas. Perhaps these, too, are not surprising in the domain of human affairs, but as they have far-reaching consequences for the management of industrial society, and possibly for its future development, it is well that we should pause from time to time to examine current theologies and seek a better understanding of their implications.

This book is a collection of essays on some of the topics alluded to. It is not intended in any sense as a systematic or comprehensive treatment of current thinking on major problems in the management field; it merely reflects my concern with each topic at the time of writing about it, so that each essay may be regarded as an entity, although a common theme may run through many presented here. Some of the issues raised are undoub-tedly controversial, and the views expressed in these essays may generate a wide spectrum of reactions. My purpose and hope is that the essays will stimulate thought and debate, and if as a result some readers feel that they have a better appreciation of the topics in question, then my efforts will have been amply rewarded.

Most of the essays appear here in their original form; some have been rewritten or modified. I am grateful to the editors of the *Operational Research Quarterly* and of *Management Science* for permission to include here four of my papers published in those journals (chapters 13 and 16 were published in the former, 9 and a shorter version of 14 in the latter); most of the others appeared as editorials in *Omega, The International Journal of Management Science.*

SAMUEL EILON

CHAPTER 1

The Board – Functions and Structure

INTRODUCTION

A great deal of attention has been focused recently on company boards, their functions and responsibilities, their composition and structure. The practice of the two-tier board in Germany is often quoted as the most significant model for organizing the company board, although this model is by no means unique, and certain variations on the theme are commonly found in other countries such as Holland and France. These experiences have led to discussions within the CEC (the Council of the European Communities) as to whether all the countries in the Common Market should adopt a single approach to the organization of the board, as proposed in the widely argued "Fifth Directive" of the CEC [1].

A major weakness in many discussions about the structure of the board is that they start by considering its composition: How many members should it have? Which functions or operations should be represented on it? How many non-executive directors should be recruited, and from where? How many worker representatives, if any, should serve on the board? All these are, of course, legitimate and important considerations, since the board is a collection of individuals who have to act together, and questions about the composition of the board must be resolved with great delicacy and care. But before looking at its composition, it is relevant to delineate the tasks that the board is expected to perform.

1

RESPONSIBILITIES OF THE BOARD

The board of directors of a company is entrusted with the responsibility of acting in the interest of that company. The question that arises is what is meant by "interest" and by "company". One view (supported by legal definitions) is that "a company is a 'company-of-shareholders' " [2, p. 10]; others would argue that the company also encompasses its employees, and that apart from responsibilities to its shareholders the board has responsibilities to its employees, to its customers, to its suppliers, and to society at large.

If the interests of the parties concerned are associated with increased material wealth and general well-being, it follows that conflicts of interest may well arise, particularly when decisions have to be made about the distribution of profits and the disposition of financial resources in the short term and in the long term [5]. Thus, apart from having to ensure the company's survival, the board needs to act in a way that will provide the desired financial resources for investment and for distribution purposes. It is this composite responsibility that needs to be borne in mind in any discussion of the board's functions and its composition.

Any managerial task, at whatever level, may be regarded as a closed-loop control process, in which the controller (= the manager) monitors operations in the system for which he is responsible and takes action from time to time to adjust various parameters that determine the behaviour and the performance of the system. For a closed-loop control process to be operative, the following ingredients are essential [3, p. 17]:

- a goal, or a standard
- a measurement task
- a feedback signal
- a control procedure
- a corrective action

For which of these ingredients (sometimes called "the controls") the manager-controller is made responsible is an organizational matter. His primary function may be confined to taking corrective action when required, namely when he perceives that the system deviates too widely from its charted course; but the charting of this course, the determination of how to measure and monitor performance, how to report about it, and under what circumstances his intervention would be expected—all these need not necessarily be part of his responsibility and may be established by higher authority, particularly when questions of co-ordination and compatibility of performance of various parts of the enterprise are of substance.

The control framework determines whether the manager's primary function is to lead the system or merely to respond to it. At the lower end of the managerial hierarchy the primary concern is that of timely response: the controller's task is to keep the system going and to respond efficiently to events within the bounds of his authority and capabilities. The frequency of his intervention and the magnitude of the corrective action that he undertakes are the major determinants of his role as a controller, and the degree to which these are flexible or prescriptive (largely from above) may characterize the management style at that organizational level.

Ultimately, the control responsibility rests with the board. The buck stops there. The board must determine the organizational structure of the enterprise and the mechanisms for controlling it. For the lower echelons in the hierarchy, the board may be content to outline a broad control framework and not to concern itself with minute details. But as far as the tasks of the board itself are concerned and its own decision processes, it needs to design the control mechanisms with great care in order to ensure that the board does not merely respond to events but has the capability to anticipate them and to shape the future of the enterprise.

Clearly, the enterprise needs direction; without it activities are bound to become unco-ordinated, purposeless, even at variance with one another. And it is the direction of the enterprise that the board should be first and foremost concerned with.

The authority-execution-feedback process may be loosely described by the inverted pyramid shown in Fig. 1.1. Each stage in this process affects or determines the next one, and feedback is essential for the process to be truly dynamic and adaptive. First, the board must determine the policy and objectives of the enterprise, choose the strategy by which these objectives should be achieved, and determine the resources to be used for the purpose. As operations proceed, sets of control mechanisms come into action to measure, to monitor, and to adjust these operations, and then a global evaluation exercise needs to be undertaken periodically to examine the performance of the enterprise, its structure, and its procedures.

The first four elements—*policy, objective setting, strategy delineation,* and *corporate planning*—may generally be regarded as the *programming* activity of the board, with *controls* and *evaluations* as the *appraisal* activity. It might be said that where programming looks forward, appraisal looks backward; but such a distinction is an oversimplification, since programming and appraisal must be interdependent. No appraisal is possible without reference to prior planning and to specified expectations; and no planning can be effective if it does not take account of past lessons. Thus, controls feed information into corporate plans, which may have to be updated and modified, while evaluation exercises feed back into the examination of the corporate ethos and the formulation of policies, objectives, and strategies.

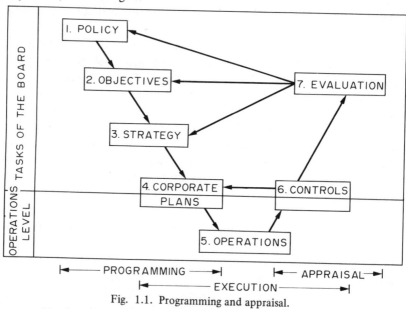

Fig. 1.1. Programming and appraisal.

Clearly, the board must take full responsibility for this total process, but what parts of it should be regarded as direct tasks of the board itself? Decisions on policies, objectives, and strategies cannot be delegated, nor can decisions following evaluation exercises. The board may seek assistance in carrying out these tasks through special board committees or groups appointed by the board for the purpose, and such assistance could be particularly relevant in data collection and analysis of alternative courses of action, for example in the examination of special projects. But the ultimate responsibility and *active* involvement in decisions on these issues must rest with the board.

The degree to which corporate planning and controls should be regarded as tasks of the board is a matter for organizational design. While the board remains responsible for corporate plans, various details may be left to personnel at the operations level, who would then have to design and implement the concomitant controls, hence Fig. 1.1 has a line that runs through the boxes marked 4 and 6 to divide them between the board and the operating level, although this dividing line should in no way be regarded as an attempt to define rigid demarcations.

POLICY AND OBJECTIVES

First, the enterprise must have a *policy*. A policy is a statement by the board, designed to provide general guidelines for management actions. Its purpose is to define the kind of business that the enterprise is engaged in, the type of products or services it aims to provide, the section of the market it should be concerned with, and the position it aspires to attain in relation to its competitors. A policy statement should also specify attitudes to growth, to diversification (of products and markets), to relations with external interests (governmental, environmental, consumer), and to the distribution of profits.

A policy statement may be timeless in that it need not indicate when certain aspirations are to be achieved, but it provides the managerial hierarchy with an essential framework of guidance for action.

Secondly, an enterprise must have specified *objectives*. The difference between policy and objectives is that the former is a general statement of intent, whereas the latter are statements about desired performance results, and this means that objectives must be:

- measurable
- quantified
- time-based
- feasible

For example, statements such as "Sales volume should increase by 15% during the next twelve months", or "Overhauls should be reduced by 10% over the next two years", may be regarded as objectives.

The purpose of specifying objectives is to provide a foundation on which activities of the enterprise can be planned and to define a yardstick against which future performance can be evaluated. The prime purpose of objective setting and planning is to map out the future activities of the enterprise and its constituent parts. If you do not know where you are going, how would you know if you have arrived? And if you do not know what route you should take, how do you know if you are on the right road? This is why objectives need to be *measurable, quantified,* and *time-based.* Thus, "to improve performance" is not an objective, since the statement does not tell us how performance is to be measured, what level of (measurable) improvement is aimed at, and over what period of time.

The specification of a measure could be implicit or it may need to be explicit, depending on how well it is understood and used in the organization. For example, "sales" are usually measured by their monetary value, and if this is the accepted measure in a given firm, no further elaboration is required. But if one of the objectives is to be associated with improving morale, it would be necessary to describe how the improvement is to be ascertained (say, by reduction in labour turnover and/or absenteeism, or by results of an attitude survey). And having established that the objective is indeed measurable, it is then necessary to quantify the desirable level of change within a specified time span. If one of these three attributes is missing (that objectives be *measurable, quantified,* and *time-based*), the statements that purport to describe objectives become meaningless for the purpose of planning and evaluating the performance of the enterprise.

I mentioned earlier that objectives should also be *feasible. Objectives are performance targets,* which may be regarded as *norms* for future reference, and there are three schools of thought on this issue, suggesting that objectives should be:

- *tight,* to stretch people
- *slack,* or "realistic", for everyone to achieve
- *open-ended* ("do the best you can")

Those who believe in tight objectives argue that demanding tasks present a challenge and are always conducive to improving performance. This is beneficial both to the enterprise and to the individual, to the former because of its enhanced competitive posture, and to the latter because of the satisfaction of achievement and pride in rising to the challenge. The philosophy of tight objectives encourages the "crawling peg" phenomenon [3, p. 188], namely the tendency to take past performance for granted and to set ever-increasing demands on future activities, leading at times to frustration, helplessness, and negative response from those involved. The question also arises "How tight is tight?" If the targets are too ambitious and the probability of attaining them is too low, they may well fall into disrepute, and once they are disregarded they become worthless.

The opposite approach to tight objectives is what some would call "realistic" objectives, having sufficient slack to allow everyone to attain satisfactory performance without much difficulty. This approach reduces the probability of failure, it also provides little or no challenge to potential high performers and may thereby miss opportunities to improve the performance of the organization as a whole. Thus, tight objectives may be regarded as conducive to breeding "thrusters", while slack objectives sustain "sleepers" [7].

The third approach is the open-ended guideline: "Do the best you can." It allows the objectives to be decentralized, so that people on the spot can make a judgement as to how much they should exert themselves in the light of prevailing circumstances. This open-ended approach is naturally very attractive to those who believe in "self-actualizing" [6], namely in allowing people to develop at their own pace with self-imposed work disciplines and achievement aspirations. In an environment where everyone can benefit from self-actualizing and where the activities of one individual neither affect nor are affected by others, this is clearly a laudable philosophy. But an industrial enterprise is often a complex web of inter-linked and inter-dependent activities, and it simply will not do for one individual or department to pursue relentlessly certain objectives and completely ignore the possible consequences to other parts of the organization. What, for example, is the point of a production department significantly increasing its output if the sales department is content to limit its sales effort, or a research and development department pursuing projects that have no chance of producing marketable products?[1]

It is clear, therefore, that each of the three philosophies, if taken to the extreme, can become inoperative or even harmful. Objectives that are too tight may fall into disuse, those that are too slack may lead to abuse, and those that are too open-ended may result in both, through lack of coordi-

---

[1] See also Chapter 5.

nation and control. A compromise is desirable: objectives that present
some challenge and yet are regarded as feasible, sufficiently definitive to
allow individual activities to be fitted into a coherent and purposeful programme, yet not so prescriptive as to stifle initiative and eliminate all room
for manoeuvre.

To some extent this problem reflects the debate between optimizing
and satisficing, although the former is much more prescriptive than is
perhaps implied by the "do the best you can" dictum (optimization involves
doing the best that *can* be done, often following certain specified procedures [3, p. 170]), while satisficing requires minimum predetermined levels
of performance to be met but allows these levels to be exceeded or for
performance to fluctuate within given limits. It is also relevant to mention
that constraints fall into this category as there is no fundamental
difference between objectives (of the non-optimal type) and constraints[2]
except that it may be convenient to describe objectives as a series of "do"s
and constraints as a series of "don't"s.

STRATEGY, CORPORATE PLANNING AND EXECUTION

The next task is to determine the way in which available resources—or
new resources—should be used in order to ensure that objectives are
achieved. Several alternative courses of action have to be examined before
a *strategy* is adopted, with the *corporate planning* activity providing a
detailed schedule of operations.

The difference between *strategy planning* and *corporate planning* lies
in the degree of detail. The first is more global and is often concerned
with a longer time scale than the latter, which gets down to a clear statement as to who does what and when and with what resources (such as
finance, materials, equipment, and manpower). The corporate plan includes
specifications of various targets (emanating from the stated objectives)
that need to be attained by predetermined dates, and these provide the
necessary yardsticks for measuring corporate performance.

As stated earlier, the selection of strategy and corporate planning are also
the responsibilities of the board, although the task of data collection, com-
putation, analysis, and the drawing up of detailed plans is often delegated to

---

[2] See also Chapter 13.

a corporate planning group under the supervision of a board member.

These are followed (Fig. 1.1) by the operations that the enterprise is engaged in—namely, the translation of plans into action—and by the setting up of control mechanisms to monitor progress and to feed the necessary information to the appropriate echelons in the management hierarchy for corrective action to be taken as and when required. It is the responsibility of the board to evaluate these control mechanisms from time to time, to update them, or to devise new ones, and to ensure that lessons from the evaluation exercise are fed into the planning process and permeate through the organizational structure.

THE TWO BOARDS

Thus, the functions of the board may conveniently be divided into two categories: the first is that of *direction,* where the board is concerned with policies, objectives, and evaluation; the second is that of *management,* where the board is charged with the responsibility of translating objectives into tangible plans (Fig. 1.2). A graphical description of the distribution

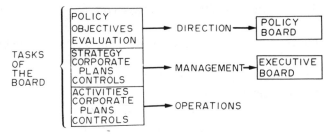

Fig. 1.2. Tasks of the board

of functions between the two boards and the operating level is given in Fig. 1.3. This does not purport to have any quantitative connotations regarding the allocation of the tasks involved; it is merely a general indication—and a crude one at that—regarding the points of emphasis and whose main concern they are. The policy board is solely concerned with policy and primarily with objective setting and evaluation, while the executive board's responsibility for strategy delineation is shared with the policy board and for corporate planning with the operating level. These and other overlaps merely reflect the involvement by the various levels already referred to in Fig. 1.1 and the necessary degree of consultation that needs to take place.

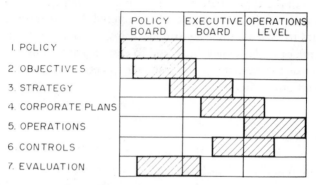

Fig. 1.3. Functions and responsibilities.

It is this fundamental difference between direction and management that provides the *raison d'être* for those who advocate splitting the board into two: a *policy board* and an *executive board,* with a hierarchical relationship between them, and it is to emphasize this hierarchy that the first is often referred to as the *supervisory board* and the latter as the *management board.*[3] While such a structure does not preclude the possibility that some individuals may serve on both boards,[4] the overlap in membership must necessarily be limited if the functions of the two are to remain essentially distinct.

The hierarchical nature of the two-tier board inevitably leads people to regard the supervisory board as the superior body and therefore as more authoritative, more powerful, and more important than the management board. Indeed, the CEC Fifth Directive goes to great lengths to stress the authority of the supervisory board:

[3]These boards may be described as "an organ responsible for controlling the management body" and "a management organ responsible for managing the business of the company" respectively [1, Preamble].

[4]This is an important point to make, although the Fifth Directive states categorically that "no person may be at the same time a member of the management organ and of the supervisory organ" [1, Article 6].

"The authorization of the supervisory organ shall be obtained for decisions of the management organ relating to:

(a) the closure or transfer of the undertaking or of substantial parts thereof;

(b) substantial curtailment or extension of the activities of the undertaking;

(c) substantial organizational changes within the undertaking;

(d) establishment of long-term co-operation with other undertakings or the termination thereof"

and further specifies that "the supervisory organ or one third of the members thereof shall be entitled to obtain from the management organ all information and relevant documents and to undertake all such investigations as may be necessary" and "the members of the management organ may be dismissed by the supervisory organ" [1, Articles 11–13].

In order to remove this rigid hierarchical connotation and to emphasize the need for the two boards to work together, the term *two-part board* was coined, the relationships between the two boards being as depicted in Fig. 1.4. Whether the fact that the two are connected in the diagram horizontally is sufficient—at least psychologically—to suggest that they have equal status, is somewhat doubtful, but it is possible to enhance such an impression by insisting that the two boards have a joint legal responsibility and operate as two parts of the same board. Clearly, there is room here for many variations on the theme to suit the environment and the specific needs of individual enterprises.

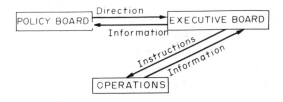

Fig. 1.4. The two-part board.

COMPOSITION AND COMMUNICATION

A conventional single board of a company usually consists of the chairman, the managing director (or chief executive), heads of operating divisions, heads of functions (such as finance, personnel, marketing, production, administration), and some non-executive directors. Thus, the majority of the full-time directors have a dual role: as directors of the enterprise they are responsible for the company as a whole, for its long-term future, and for its performance; as heads of operating units or functions they tend to act as representatives of their departments or divisions, to look after their sectional interests, and often to be concerned with the short term.

This dual role is bound to generate conflicts of interests. A divisional head, whose daily concern is to ensure that operations under his control proceed smoothly and to look after the welfare of his men, is required to forget his immediate problems and to concentrate on long-term issues the minute he walks into the boardroom, and it is not surprising that many directors are constantly faced with agonizing decisions when they have to operate in this dual role capacity.

The two-part board does not eliminate this dilemma, but it certainly helps to defuse what may otherwise become very difficult situations by essentially segregating those responsible for operating divisions and functions—and assigning them to the executive board—from those concerned with the long-term future of the enterprise, who are not deeply involved in the day-to-day running of its constituent parts—and assigning them to the policy board.

This would result in the policy board consisting of the chairman and the non-executive directors, with the managing director also taking part and providing the policy board with all the necessary information to evaluate the performance of the company and to make decisions of a major character such as on large capital expenditure, mergers and acquisitions, strategic realignment of resources, or new ventures. The policy board is also responsible for the approval of the annual accounts, preferably at a joint meeting with the executive board, to emphasize the joint legal responsibility for the accounts by the two parts of the board. Senior appointments—certainly of all directors, and possibly even of senior executives one echelon below the directors' level—should also be a matter for decision by the policy board.

The membership of the executive board would then consist of the heads of operating divisions and functions with the managing director in the chair but without any of the outside directors. Because the executive board is so concerned with day-to-day operations, it is likely to meet more frequently than the policy board, certainly once a month and possibly more often.

The question of overlapping membership is a delicate one. At one end of the spectrum, where the overlap is complete and everyone is a member of both boards, there is a danger that the distinction between direction and management is obliterated, a problem that has already been alluded to earlier. At the other end, where the boards are mutually exclusive [1] and where the managing director is the only common member (perhaps in a reporting capacity as far as the supervisory board is concerned), there is a danger of inadequate, perhaps even biased, information flow between the two boards; the fact that some directors may perceive the information as biased—irrespective of whether such a perception is justified or not—may result in some mutual distrust, with the non-executive directors wondering whether they are getting the whole truth about past and current events, while full-time executive directors tend to complain that their non-executive colleagues are somewhat remote and do not share their problems and anxieties.

These difficulties can be overcome in two ways—first through appropriate procedures, and, secondly, with increased joint membership. The first may include the following:

- a joint meeting of the two boards to approve the annual accounts, and perhaps a similar joint meeting to review half-yearly progress
- minutes and other documents of the executive board to be circulated to all members of the policy board
- at each meeting of the policy board a member of the executive board to make a presentation about a particular major problem, or to review progress of activities under his responsibility.

Such procedures will facilitate smooth communication between the two parts of the board and will provide opportunities for personal contacts. As for a wider overlap of membership, the obvious solutions that can be adopted are:

- the chairman becoming a member of the executive board (this will ensure that he becomes less isolated from the rest of the enterprise) though not necessarily having to attend every meeting
- one or two members of the executive board becoming members of the policy board for *a limited time period* (this will ensure that a better appreciation of policy issues permeates through to the executive board)

All these measures are designed to provide a framework for harmonious relationships between the two boards and at the same time to emphasize that each has its own role to play; this is perhaps the major difference between the two-part board and the two-tier board philosophies, the latter being so vividly exemplified by the very rigid definitions and "at-arms-length" dealings proposed by the CEC Fifth Directive. Such rigidity is perhaps inevitable when attempts are made to resolve organizational problems by a legislative machinery, but no board can realize its full potential without its members having a modicum of mutual trust and a common purpose, and these can only be enhanced in an environment in which free exchange of information is encouraged.

NON-EXECUTIVE DIRECTORS

It is apposite to highlight in this context the important role of the non-executive directors who can make a valuable contribution not only by reason of their wider knowledge and experience outside the company but by their objectivity [2, p. 37]. Because they have no axe to grind and because they are not involved in the day-to-day management of the company, they can afford to take a detached view of the issues brought before the board and to make an independent assessment of its policy and alternative courses of action.

Non-executive directors need to be thoughtfully selected with more care than some current haphazard procedures appear to suggest. The casual way in which such directors are sometimes recruited is quite incompatible with a responsible attitude towards the board's functions and often leads to a lamentable diminution of the potential contribution that the non-executive directors can make. To allow this contribution to materialize, the non-executive directors must be made to feel that they share in the responsibility for the direction of the enterprise, and they must be given adequate facilities to become fully acquainted with the company's operations and its top executives.

THE EVALUATION PROCESS

Finally, let us return to a central task of the board, that of evaluation. No objective setting, no planning, no decision making can be effective without feedback and evaluation, and it is an important function of the board to ensure that a series of analyses is undertaken and updated from time to time to form the basis for discussion about the company's future operations and about the need for change in its structure and in the deployment of its resources. Such analyses are performed as a matter of course in some companies' planning departments,[5] but it is important to ensure that they are carried out on behalf of the board, that they are regularly reported to the board, and that they are not relegated to an obscure part of the organization.

These evaluation exercises should cover a wide range of topics, many of which may well overlap:

1. *Performance analysis.* How does performance compare with objectives and expectations? Given hindsight, how should the company have acted and used its resources better? What lessons can one learn about the setting of objectives for the future?

2. *Control analysis.* How do the control mechanisms operate? Does the board get the right kind of information? Is the reporting and feedback information relevant, accurate, and available in time for action to be taken when required? Is there too much redundant paperwork in the system? Are the measures of performance appropriate, and how can they be modified to improve the quality of information for future evaluation of objectives and performance?

3. *Economic analysis.* What do the economic/political forecasts at home and abroad imply to the company's future operations? In what way should they affect investment decisions, the opening of new plants, or the planning of joint ventures with other companies?

[5] See, for example, [8].

4. *Strengths and weaknesses analysis.* What are the main strengths of the company in relation to its competitors and to the market place? What are its major resources? Where it is lacking in strength, and where is it vulnerable?

5. *Competitor analysis.* What strategies can competitors adopt to exploit their own strengths which would impinge on the company's operations and future standing?

6. *Diversification and growth analysis.* What is the potential of various markets and should the company try to increase its market share? Should it diversify its products, services, or markets? What would the implications be of such policies on the company's resources, on its structure, and on research and development programmes?

7. *Customers, suppliers, and environmental analysis.* What do customers think of the company? Are they getting value for money, and can feedback procedures be established to provide effective information from the market place? Are the suppliers reliable, and what would be the consequences if some supply lines broke down? Does the company generate negative societal reaction by reason of pollution, noise, congestion, or other causes? How can the company make a useful contribution to the locality in which it operates and to society at large?

8. *Manpower analysis.* Does the company have the right "stock" of people, in terms of quality and quantity, to meet present and future challenges? How can recruitment be improved? Are procedures for career planning, training, and assessment of potential sufficiently effective? How do salaries and remunerations compare with other companies and industries?

9. *Takeover analysis.* Is the company vulnerable to a takeover bid, from what quarter, and for what reasons? What would the consequences be for the enterprise, and how could the board react? Similarly, what opportunitites for takeovers of other companies exist, and what strategies should be considered for the purpose?

10. *Scenario analysis.* The method of scenario building can be very effective in testing the company's capability to meet new chal-

lenges or to exploit new opportunities. A given scenario may emphasize drastic changes in the economic/political climate, in credit controls, in demand, in supply of raw materials, in technology. How would the company react to such changes, and would it be flexible and agile enough to cope with a dynamic and volatile environment?

These are some examples of evaluation exercises that the board should be concerned with, but the emphasis will vary depending on the nature of the enterprise and its products or services. A company that is highly technical in its orientation may have technical matters brought to the board, such as strategies of research and development, product design, or even methods of manufacture. Other company boards may spend an inordinate amount of time on marketing strategies, advertising, financial problems, or industrial relations.

What every board must do is to evaluate itself, its composition and procedures, its information system, and its decision-making processes. It needs to ensure that time is spent on issues that matter, that it does not waste effort on trivialities, and that it does not suck away effective authority from the management hierarchy.

CONCLUSION

An important observation that must be made in discussing the organization of the board is that there is no single formula by which it can be described. As we have seen, the single board, the two-tier board, and the two-part board are manifestations of differing views about the tasks and responsibilities of individual directors, about corporate responsibility, and about participation, but any particular viewpoint does not necessarily imply a single definitive structure. There are many variations on the theme, in terms of the board composition, the length of service of its members, the frequency of meetings, the demarcation of responsibilities (below the board and between boards, when a two-tier or two-part board system is adopted), the exchange of information and feedback, the extent of the evaluation process undertaken on its behalf, and the level of detailed control to be exercised. Every enterprise is unique; it operates in an environment with specific characteristics that may be very different from that of another enterprise, even in the same industry. Thus, a board designed for one company may not necessarily suit another, since it is not only the external environment that affects the way in which an enterprise is organized, but also its internal milieu, and the attitudes and aspirations of its members with respect to profit, to the corporate ethos, and to participation.

REFERENCES

1. Commission of the European Communities (1972) *Proposal for a Fifth Directive on the Structure of Sociétés Anonymes,* Bulletin of the European Communities, supplement 10/72.
2. Confederation of British Industry (1973) *The Responsibilities of the British Public Company* (final report of the Company Affairs Committee).
3. Eilon, S. (1971) *Management Control,* Macmillan, London.
4. Eilon, S. (1972) Goals and constraints in decision-making, *Operational Research Quarterly,* vol. 23, no. 1, pp. 3 - 15; also in Chapter 13 of this book.
5. Eilon, S. (1973) On the corporate ethos, *Foundation for Business Responsibilities,* London; also *Omega,* vol. 1, no. 4, pp, 393 - 6, 1973; a modified version is included in this book in Chapter 6.
6. Maslow, A. H. (1954) *Motivation and Personality,* Harper & Row.
7. Political and Economic Planning (1965) *Thrusters and Sleepers,* Allen & Unwin.
8. Springer, C. H. (1973) Strategic management in General Electric, *Operations Research,* vol. 21, no. 6, pp. 1177 - 82.

CHAPTER 2

Worker Participation

Man is a social animal. He rarely works on his own, and as a member of an organization he continuously interacts with other people, with superiors, with subordinates, and with equals. His work, let alone his attitude, is bound to be affected by these interactions, since organizational procedures that impinge on his task determine the specifications of his role and responsibilities.

It is not surprising, therefore, that a great deal of attention has been devoted in recent years—by writers on organization theory, by politicians, and by the press—to the question of worker participation in the industrial enterprise to which he belongs. Some attitudes to participation are admirably summarized by McGregor, who says [5, pp. 124 - 5]:

"Participation is one of the most misunderstood ideas that have emerged from the field of human relations. It is praised by some, condemned by others, and used with considerable success by still others. The differences in point of view between its proponents and its critics are about as great as those between the leaders of Iron Curtain countries and those of the Free World when they use the term 'democracy'.

"Some proponents of participation give the impression that it is a magic formula which will eliminate conflict and disagreement and come pretty close to solving all of managements' problems. These enthusiasts appear to believe that people yearn to participate . . . that it is a formula which can be applied by any manager regardless of his skill, that virtually no preparation is necessary for its use, and that it can spring full-blown into existence and transform industrial relationships overnight.

"Some critics of participation, on the other hand, see it as a form of managerial abdication. It is a dangerous idea that will undermine managerial prerogatives and almost certainly get out of control. . . . It wastes time, lowers efficiency, and weakens management's effectiveness.

"A third group of managers views participation as a useful item in their bag of managerial tricks. It is for them a manipulative device for getting people to do what they want, under conditions that delude the 'participators' into thinking they have had a voice in decision making. . . . A fourth group of managers makes successful use of participation, but they don't think of it as a panacea or magic formula. They do not share either the unrestrained enthusiasm of the faddists or the fears of the critics."

McGregor proceeds to point out that all these approaches—incorrectly in his view—are concerned with participation of groups and not of individuals; also, they do not regard participation as having any relationship to delegation, whereas he contends that "the effective use of participation is a consequence of a managerial point of view which includes confidence in the potentialities of subordinates . . . . and a desire to avoid some of the negative consequences of emphasis on personal authority" [5, pp. 126 - 7].

One particular aspect of participation which has been widely talked about recently is that of worker-directors. Because of the German experience with the two-tier board system, in which there are worker representatives on the supervisory board, and because of the Fifth Directive of the Common Market Commission, which advocates such a structure and specifies that at least "one third of the members of the supervisory organ shall be appointed by the workers or their representatives or upon proposal by the workers or their representatives" [1, Article 4], it is often assumed in discussions on the two-tier or two-part board structure that it involves worker participation and, furthermore, that it automatically involves worker-directors on the board.[1] In fact, the questions of two-tier boards and of worker-directors

---

[1] For example, the Confederation of British Industry (CBI) Report states that the concept of two-tier boards "may well have arisen from a desire to secure better methods of employee participation in industrial decision making and as such is to be welcomed, but it does not offer an acceptable solution to British practice" [2, p. 20].

are two separate issues: it is possible to have a single board with worker-directors on it, and a two-tier board without any, although the presence or otherwise of worker-directors is bound to affect boardroom procedures, as, indeed, is the presence of other powerful board members with strong views and convictions.

WORKER PARTICIPATION

Participation may be seen as a wide spectrum of possible levels of involvement, as discussed by Likert [4, p. 243]. In the process of decision making the spectrum may cover the following:

- no information is given to employees, all tasks are highly prescriptive
- limited information is given to explain the background for highly prescriptive tasks
- a fair amount of information is given, but tasks remain prescriptive
- information is provided and employees are asked to comment on proposed actions
- information and problems are defined and employees are asked to propose solutions for management to choose from
- problems are solved jointly by management and employees within constraints imposed by both sides
- problems are jointly defined, thereby involving employee participation in setting the objectives of the enterprise and questioning constraints
- solutions allow a fair measure of decentralized decisions and local personalistic control.

This scale may apply both at the level of the individual and the level of the group, and clearly the two may not be compatible. An opportunity for the individual to define and solve problems relating to his workplace or personal welfare may be in conflict with the participation process of group of employees concerned with the same problems or with dependent activities.

Participation may be considered along two separate dimensions (Fig. 2.1). The first is associated with the fruits of the enterprise and involves participation in profits or even ownership through a variety of schemes:

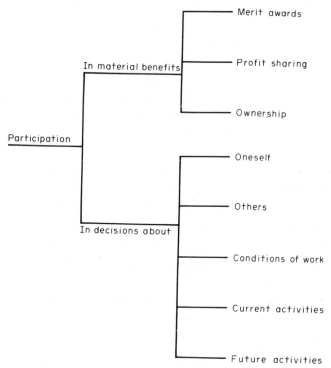

Fig. 2.1. Facets of participation.

from merit awards to acknowledge the contribution of individuals, to a given proportion of the annual profit set aside for employees (distributed in cash in proportion to employees' wages or salaries, or put into an investment fund in which each employee has a stake encashable after some specified period), to trappings of ownership (by share allocation, or by opportunities to purchase shares at attractive terms). The second dimension of participation is concerned with power sharing, namely with mechanisms that allow employees to be involved in the decision-making processes in the firm (Fig. 2.1). Such participation may centre on the individual, relating to decisions affecting his job specifications, remuneration, career prospects, promotion, and transfer, the physical environment of his workplace; it may involve an individual in decisions affecting others, such as in job evaluation, assessment of performance, merit awards, selection, and determination of future prospects; it may relate to general conditions of work, physical and social amenities during and after working hours; it may focus on current production methods, schedules, manning problems, layout, inventory, and quality control; and, finally, participation may involve people taking part in discussions about future operations— launching new products, diversification, changes in production methods, investment in new plant, marketing and pricing strategies, reorganization, and so on.

All the facets of participation are not mutually exclusive. As suggested earlier, decisions affecting the position of any single person in the organization may have repercussions on others; similarly, it is rarely possible to separate discussions of schedules and production methods from their possible effects on people (and vice versa). Figure 2.1 is not intended as a list of issues to be regarded as watertight compartments, but as a general indication of the main points of emphasis. And, clearly, these modes of worker participation form a very wide spectrum, and reactions to them are bound to be varied: for example, share allocation to employees is applauded by some as a means of achieving true co-ownership, while others argue that it is not in the employee's interest to have his capital tied up in his own company and cite examples of employees losing both jobs and savings when their companies were in difficulties or collapsed; some warmly welcome the principle of profit sharing, others fear that bonuses would readily become expected as part of normal remuneration; voting rights without share holding is strongly argued as a means of accepting the principle that employees should have a similar voice to that of shareholders in approving the board's actions and in electing its members, although the distribution of voting power between employees and shareholders is a matter on which many will disagree.

Each scheme of participation implies its own level of commitment on the part of management, the individual employee, and the population of employees as a whole in the enterprise; each scheme can be handled either by statute through legal provisions or by voluntary *ad hoc* arrangements.

In discussing the merits or advisability of participation it is essential to ask: What is it for and what is it designed to achieve?

Those who argue that the main object of participation is to improve the material well-being of employees will concentrate on profit sharing and bonus schemes. Those who regard employee participation as a means of improving the efficiency of the enterprise will set up a consultative machinery in the form of works councils and/or planning committees. Those who believe in the right of employees to own the enterprise (at least in part) and to chart its long-term future will argue for transfer of ownership and for worker representation on the board. Those who are anxious to safeguard the individual's position will strive to ensure that any participation formula to promote group decision making and worker representation in any form does not deprive the individual of the opportunity to be involved in decisions affecting his future.

Thus, the motives of those advocating worker participation vary enormously. No doubt many strongly believe that participation offers the best means of abating industrial unrest, reducing conflict between management and the workforce, and instilling a sense of identification of the individual within the organization. In this way, they argue, a positive incentive is provided to meet targets, to undertake new responsibilities, to face change, and to promote innovation. Others are less interested in this pragmatic approach; for them the true test of participation is not whether it does improve the performance of the enterprise or not, but whether it offers the workers the power to affect their own welfare and destiny, although how one measures the differences in tangible results between the pragmatists and the idealists in this context is not at all clear, particularly as not all facets of participation can be expected to have the same effects, and not all are universally applicable or even relevant to all industrial firms. It is, therefore, a salutary exercise for any proposed scheme for participation, to delineate its various objectives, and to ascertain the extent to which some can be achieved, perhaps at the expense of others.

It is also important to realize the multiple effect of participation by legislation. On the one hand, it can provide a framework within which employees can be assured of their right to be involved in whatever form is prescribed, a right that they can exercise and which cannot be denied to them by any authoritative management. But true participation requires mutual confidence. It requires management to believe that the participatory process is beneficial to the enterprise and that employees have a right to know, to be consulted, and to be involved in managerial activities. It requires employees to realize that their participation involves responsibility, the ability to look at the needs of the enterprise as a whole, and a determination not to pursue relentlessly sectional interests. It is precisely this level of mutual understanding and the local consensus of what participation is designed to achieve that is very difficult to cover by a legislative framework, and there is always a danger that predetermined participation formats, set on a static rather than a dynamic pattern, may become organizationally ossified into rigid lines of demarcation and rituals of power conflict and confrontation.

CO-DETERMINATION AND WORKER-DIRECTORS

The term "co-determination" is now often used to describe the involvement of workers in the decision-making process in Germany, although—as Fogarty points out— "the word *Mitbestimmung*, besides its precise legal significance, has a much looser popular meaning covering practically any form of employee participation, including areas of negotiation and of joint consultation which in principle at least are entirely uncontroversial", and he proceeds to define co-determination "to mean a right for employees, or their representatives, to share in the ultimate authority within a firm, that which appoints and discusses the firm's chief executives and calls them to account" and, further, he concentrates "on the case where employee representatives share in the firm's ultimate power at least on an equal footing with those who supply the firm's capital . . . with or without the further presence of representatives of consumers and the public interest" [3, p. 5].

Defined in this way, co-determination is largely concerned with power sharing and industrial democracy, with the right of an employee to have an effective voice in shaping present and future activities of the enterprise in which he works. This needs to be contrasted with other forms of employee participation referred to earlier: the right to be informed and consulted, the right to take part in decision making at the tactical and shop-floor level, the right to profit sharing, and the right to take part and vote (with or without share holding) at annual and extraordinary general meetings.

There is no question that a greater level of worker participation than that currently experienced in most western countries is desirable, indeed overdue, and this is now generally accepted,[2] not just because of impending legislative machinery and trade union pressures, but because employees' intrinsic rights and responsibilities at their place of work are more widely recognized. There is certainly a need to devise formulae that will allow worker participation, where appropriate, in decision-making, in consultative organs, in profit sharing, and in voting rights[3] —and new experiments on these lines should be embarked upon.

UNITY OF PURPOSE OF THE BOARD

But the question of worker-directors centres on a very vexed issue: Should an individual be appointed as a director because of his inherent qualities, his professional abilities, his experience, his potential contribution to the firm as a whole? Or should he act as a delegate representing specific sectional interests?

The concept of a worker-director can only be interpreted in the context of the latter, since an individual capable of making a contribution in his own right would generally have the normal channels of selection and promotion available to him. But when a worker-director is a representative of some or all employees, where does his loyalty lie? Sverre Thon argues strongly: "A main objection to legal co-determination is the split loyalty that the representatives of the employees must become subject to as members of the board of directors. They are elected as workers' representatives and should answer to them for their behaviour on the board" [3, p. 15].

---

[2] The CBI, for example, states: "The board has to forge closer relationships with its employees towards a common purpose. This is in the interest of its shareholders as well as its employees. The main purpose must be to secure a wider participation in the processes of decision making on the part of all employees" [2, pp. 45-46]. Notice the reference to *all* employees (in contrast, presumably, to organized or unionized labour) and to the benefits to shareholders.

[3] Schemes that would allow employees without share ownership to vote at annual and extraordinary general meetings are perfectly feasible, although many questions arise regarding their relative voting power *vis-à-vis* the shareholders, and whether all employees should be given equal voting rights, irrespective of length of service and status in the organization.

That a conflict of interests would arise is inevitable: short-term benefits and gains to employees can often be obtained at the expense of benefits to other interested parties (the customers, the suppliers, the shareholders, the environ-mental amenities[4]) and as the workers' representative the worker-director is bound to pursue the interests of the employees in preference to all others.

It must be argued that a distinction should be made between a delegate and a representative. The former usually has a clear mandate; he acts as the mouthpiece for those who have elected him, and he needs to refer to them any decision or change in circumstances for a fresh mandate. The represen-tative, on the other hand, has much wider room for manoeuvre; he has the interests of his electors at heart, but he makes decisions and votes according to his own conscience, without having to seek prior approval from his elec-tors. Delegates on the board are not just a nuisance; they form a recipe for structured conflict, inaction, and interminable delays. Boards with represen-tatives are less vulnerable to partisan strife, but it does not take long before a representative is accused by his electors of abandoning their interests and of having become alien to their cause.

The German experience seems to suggest that the supervisory board is often divided, with representatives of shareholders and representatives of labour assuming diametrically opposed postures. Some students of the German industrial scene even argue that this confrontation has led to the centre of gravity—as far as strategic decisions are concerned—shifting to the management board, resulting in greater isolation and diminution of power of the supervisory board. In iron and steel firms and in the coal industry in Germany the supervisory board consists of equal numbers of shareholders' and workers' representatives, with one outside independent director (agreed upon by both sides) holding the balance. But this very high proportion of worker-directors (in most firms in Germany the representation of worker-directors until recently amounted to one-third of the supervisory board) seems to have done little to reduce the partisan cleavage of the board, only to make it more entrenched and institutionalized.

This problem of sectional representation on the board arises not only with worker-directors but with shareholders as well. When a large investor exercises his right to appoint representatives on the board to look after his

---

[4] See Chapter 6.

interests, he puts them in a similar potential conflict situation as that of
worker-directors, causing divided loyalties, possible confrontation, and
frustration.

To achieve unity of purpose, the board must be seen to act as a body,
with joint responsibility for the company as a whole, and this includes all
the interested parties within the enterprise—its shareholders and creditors,
its suppliers and customers. Decisions taken by the board need to take
account of the short-term as well as the long-term effects on all concerned.
It is by clearly and unequivocally accepting that the board has responsibilities
also to the employees, and not only to the shareholders of the company,
that the need for sectional representation on the board disappears.

This is not to say that members of the board need to agree on everything. But a board is not unlike a cabinet of ministers, where members may
have their own views as to what policies would be best to adopt, and a con-
census emerges which all members are then prepared to accept. Anyone who
feels very strongly on a particular issue and finds that a decision has gone
against his convictions, is then faced with an agonizing choice: either he re-
signs and thereby absolves himself of any responsibility for the action in question or he decides to acquiesce in the knowledge and hope that he can still
influence future events and thereby make his contribution to the company's
welfare, but then he has to accept joint responsibility with his colleagues to
all the decisions and actions of the board for as long as he continues as its
member.

The question of "joint cabinet responsibility" need not—at least in theory
—depend on the mechanism of election to the board. It is possible, for
example, for large institutional shareholders to have the right to nominate a
member to serve on the board and to select the nominee entirely on his
personal attributes without any strings attached. The nominee would then
be neither a delegate nor a representative; his actions would be dictated by
what he considered to be appropriate for the enterprise as a whole, completely unmotivated by the desires and expectations of those who nomi-
nated him. Such an outcome is perfectly possible, and the board member
in question would then be no more distinguishable from his fellow directors
than the probable distinction they have from each other. Nevertheless, it is
important to ascertain that the mechanism of election is seen to be fair and
devoid of possible sectional bias, which can only hamper the harmonious
working of the board.

REFERENCES

1. Commission of the European Communities (1972) *Proposal for a Fifth Directive on the Structure of Sociétés Anonymes,* Bulletin of the European Communities, supplement 10/72.
2. Confederation of British Industry (1973) *The Responsibilities of the British Public Company* (final report of the Company Affairs Committee).
3. Industrial Education and Research Foundation (1970) *Worker Representation on Company Boards,* discussion paper No. 2.
4. Likert, R. (1961) *New Patterns of Management,* McGraw-Hill.
5. McGregor, D. (1960) *The Human Side of Enterprise,* McGraw-Hill.

CHAPTER 3

McGregor Revisited

ON ADVOCATING A NEW FAITH

Theory X and Theory Y have become familiar terms in our common managerial language. Many consultants have cashed in on these trademarks of two seemingly opposite schools of thought regarding organizational design, and have made it their mission in life to explain the evils of the first and to propagate the promises of the second. You find even senior executives proudly pounding their chests and proclaiming in public that they are reformed Theory Y men and that their organizations are committed to Theory Y principles, where employees have a sense of harmony and mutual belonging. Listening to the disciples of Theory Y, one cannot help being struck by their faith in the ultimate healing powers of their cosmology to eradicate all the organizational ills that have been perpetrated on our industrial society by the old-fashioned and authoritarian Theory X.

It was McGregor who coined the terms Theory X and Theory Y in his classic book *The Human Side of Enterprise* [1], and we are very much in his debt for his perceptive analyses of various managerial actions and beliefs. His systematic and relentless attacks on the conventional wisdom of management theory, on the effectiveness of authority as a means of control, on the principles of hierarchical structure and unity of command, on the division between line and staff, and on the organization chart as an adequate description of organizational roles—together with an attractive style of writing and countless memorable aphorisms—have earned him an unchallenged place among the major contributors to the study of organizational behaviour.

But over the years, Theory X and Theory Y have become clichés, hardened by the vagaries of use, with debators and writers describing the two schools of thought as diametrically opposed in their perception of causality and human behaviour in organizational structures. This polarity of views was in many ways enhanced by the way in which McGregor presented his case, advocating the adoption of Theory Y in preference to Theory X and describing their respective contrasting attributes. For the benefit of those readers who have not read McGregor (and there are surprisingly many who hotly debate his views without having read him), it may be useful to summarize these attributes as he saw them.

TWO THEORIES

"Every managerial act rests on a theory" [1, p. 6]. It is only when the manager has a hypothesis or a theory regarding the behaviour of the system with which he is concerned that he is able to make sensible decisions, to prefer one course of action to others, to explain the rationality of his choices. McGregor therefore asserts that "the key question for top management is: What are your assumptions (implicit as well as explict) about the most effective way to manage people?" [1, p. vi.], and these assumptions then reflect a hypothesis of human reaction and behaviour on the basis of which a coherent exposition on how management should go about its business can be made.

This leads McGregor to describe the two theories. Under the title "Theory X: the traditional view of direction and control", he proceeds to list some "remarkably pervasive" assumptions "implicit in most literature of organization and in much current managerial policy and practice" [1, pp. 33 - 34]:

1. "The average human being has an inherent dislike of work and will avoid it if he can."

2. "Because of this human characteristic of dislike of work, most people must be coerced, controlled, directed, threatened with punishment to get them to put forth adequate effort toward the achievement of organizational objectives."

3. "The average human being prefers to be directed, wishes to avoid responsibility, has relatively little ambition, wants security above all."

He argues that "Theory X explains the *consequences* of a particular managerial strategy; it neither explains nor discusses human nature although it purports to", and he dismisses what "appear to be new strategies—decentralization, management by objectives, consultative supervision, 'democratic' leadership" as "usually old wine in new bottles, because the procedures developed to implement them are derived from the same inadequate assumptions about human nature" [p. 42].

He then contrasts Theory X with its assumptions of the "mediocrity of the masses" with "Theory Y: the interpretation of individual and organizational goals", whose assumptions are [1, pp. 47 - 48]:

1. "The expenditure of physical and mental effort in work is as natural as play or rest. The average human being does not inherently dislike work. . . ."

2. "External control and the threat of punishment are not the only means for bringing about effort towards organizational objectives. Man will exercise self-direction and self-control in the service of objectives to which he is committed."

3. "Commitment to objectives is a function of the rewards associated with their achievement. The most significant of such rewards, e.g. the satisfaction of ego and self-actualization needs, can be direct products of effort directed toward organizational objectives."

4. "The average human being learns, under proper conditions, not only to accept but to seek responsibility. . . ."

5. "The capacity to exercise a relatively high degree of imagination, ingenuity, and creativity in the solution of organizational problems is widely, not narrowly, distributed in the population."

6. "Under the conditions of modern industrial life, the intellectual potentialities of the average human being are only partially utilized."

The contrast is glaring enough, but McGregor takes every opportunity to underline it further:

"Consider a manager who holds people in relatively low esteem. He sees himself as a member of a small elite endowed with unusual capacities, and the bulk of the human race as rather limited. He believes also that most people are inherently lazy, prefer to be taken care of, desire strong leadership. He sees them as prepared to take advantage of employment relationships unless they are closely controlled and firmly directed. In short, he holds to Theory X. . . . 'Consider now a manager with a contrasting set of attitudes. . . . He regards his subordinates as genuine assets in helping him fulfil his own responsibilities and he is concerned with creating the conditions which enable him to realize these assets. He does not feel that people in general are stupid, lazy, irresponsible, dishonest or antagonistic. He is aware that there are such individuals, but he expects to encounter them only rarely. In short, he holds to Theory Y" [1, pp. 139 - 40.]

IS A MIXED COSMOLOGY POSSIBLE?

This black and white picture could not be more starkly painted, and it is not surprising that the presentation of these two contrasting theologies should have led to violent reactions from the opposing throngs of believers who rushed to defend their respective faiths, to those who proudly announce their conversion from the oppressive X to the enlightened Y, to those who confessed their beliefs in both (often proclaiming a leaning towards Y, at least in theory if not in practice).

McGregor would have none of this mixed-religious nonsense, and in his last book *The Professional Manager* [2], he reiterates many of his original arguments and asserts that he has not found it necessary in the intervening years to change his major assumptions, but he is clearly concerned about reactions to his first book, and the two theories are no longer presented as contrasting alternatives. Instead, he says that "Theory X and Y are not polar opposites; they do not lie at extremes of a scale. They are simply *different* cosmologies"; he is prepared to accept that other sets of beliefs about the nature of man "might be labeled Theory A or O or S": indeed, he goes as far as to say "It was not my intention to suggest more than that these [Theory X and Theory Y] are examples of two among many managerial cosmologies, nor to argue that the particular beliefs I listed represent the whole of either of these cosmologies" [2, p. 79], and he considers it less important to categorize cosmologies than to understand their impact on managerial strategies [2, p. 80], although how one could do the latter without the former remains unclear. This seemingly defensive posture is perhaps understandable, following the deep impression and the searching questions generated by the first book, although the alternative strategies and the managerial styles that might stem from different cosmologies do not become thereby more coherent. For example, we need to know whether it is possible for a particular cosmology to lead to several alternative strategies (McGregor is prepared to accept that the holders of Theory X "could adopt a considerable array of strategies" [2, p. 79]), or for the same strategy to be the logical outcome of non-identical cosmologies, and why. Unless we understand the relationships between a cosmology and its resultant strategy, it is meaningless to compare cosmologies or to attempt to convert believers from one to another. That this is of some practical value is evident from McGregor's own discussion of the application of Theory Y as a strategy involving four phases:

1. "The clarification of the broad requirements of the job."
2. "The establishment of specific 'targets' for a limited time period."
3. "The management process during the target period."
4. "Appraisal of the results." [1, p. 63.]

Students of control theory will readily recognize these steps as elements of a control process ("control" in the sense of target setting, measurement, feedback, appraisal, and corrective action, not in the sense of an oppressive, authoritarian, or inhuman activity), which many would claim is relevant and is widely employed, even when the manager holds to beliefs other than those demanded by Theory Y (it would apply to implementation under Theory X, for that matter). There is nothing unique in the strategy described here to identify it solely with Theory Y, although the managerial style involved will inevitably be affected by the prevailing cosmology.

Thus, McGregor's statement that cosmologies must be regarded as discrete entities which "do not lie on a continuous scale" may be contentious, although much depends on how one defines, in his context, "discrete" and "continuous". This question, and whether it is possible to have a mixed cosmology (with elements taken from already defined sets such as X and Y or others, provided the selected elements are not contradictory), is perhaps far less important than that insisted on by McGregor in his books. But the possibility that a "soft" managerial style or strategy (as McGregor calls it) emanating from Theory X may for practical purposes be indistinguishable from a strategy emanating from Theory Y does present us with intriguing methodological difficulties. This is not to say that we should abandon the study of managerial cosmologies as such, and if anything remains valid from McGregor's memorable exposition of Theory X and Theory Y it must be his sound advice that we should always explicitly state our assumptions, preferably prior to making decisions, since it is only by so doing that posterior evalua-tions or any analyses of consistency and causality can be sensibly under-taken.

ON MOTIVATION

Throughout all our discussions of managerial style, of the rigidity of organizational design and of the level of control imposed on organizational activities, runs the common theme of human motivation, and it is not surprising that McGregor should have devoted so much attention in his thesis to the extent and implication of motivation in organizational structures. Commenting on the conventional approach of management to this subject he observes that:

> "Managerial practice appears to reflect at least a tacit belief that motivating people to work is a 'mechanical' problem. There are certain similarities between this view of man at work and Newton's laws of motion. To a considerable degree, man has been perceived to be a physical body at rest. The applications of external force is required to set him in motion to motivate him to work. Consequently, extrinsic rewards and punishments are the obvious and appropriate form to be utilized in controlling organized human effort." [2, p. 8.]

It is this mechanistic concept that gave birth to time and motion study, to determine time standards for tasks, to dividing work into separate compo-nents (thereby increasing specialization and reducing overall skill), to setting up paced production lines and highly prescriptive administrative systems, to the development of wage incentive schemes. By limiting the scope for variability in human activity and confining performance to measures of output at acceptable standards of quality, a simple means for rewarding employees by results is established, but this then becomes an effective device for alienating them and for discouraging ingenuity and initiative. This much is appreciated even by the most mechanically minded Theory X believers, but their attention would be focused on the question of trade-off between the efficient and orderly working of a highly deterministic system against the loss of freedom to its constituent parts. It is at least conceivable that some manufacturing and administration systems are more appropriate to run in this way, particularly when they are placed in a certain social-political-economic environment. But even in a given environment it would be fruitless to argue that all enterprises should be run with the same managerial style or that all managers should be imbued with the same principles of a single all-pervading cosmology, and while the examples given by McGregor to demonstrate the adoption of Theory Y in practice are impressive, one can think of numerous enterprises where the strategies described would be less than appropriate.

Even within a particular enterprise, situations may arise where the adoption of new control procedures may well pose a threat or discomfort to individuals. An example quoted by McGregor highlights the way prescriptive managerial control can make serious inroads into the individual's freedom of action [1, p. 170]. He relates the case of a company with a large stock of replacement parts; a firm of consultants was called in and introduced an elaborate inventory control system, which cut investment in inventory by half. The managers thoroughly disliked the system and argued that it was wasteful; they clearly resented the curtailment of their freedom, although economic logic suggested that the new scheme was beneficial. It is not obvious how the organization should react in such cases, except to encourage the inventory control study and its implementation to be carried out with the full collaboration of the personnel concerned but the problems caused by the introduction of formal and highly prescriptive control systems are not necessarily thereby eradicated.

McGregor's concern with motivation stems from the argument of man's hierarchy of needs; at the lowest level there are physiological needs (food, rest, exercise, shelter), but when these are satisfied, other needs become predominant: the need for safety and a sense of belonging, the need for love, appreciation, status, and achievement. All these social needs are completely ignored, or hardly catered for, by conventional incentive strategies, and as "man is a wanting animal—as soon as one of his needs is satisfied, another appears in its place" [1, p. 36]. It is therefore all the more difficult to expect any static strategy, irrespective of what cosmology it is based on, to be able to cater for such a dynamic unending process. Many writers have pinned their hopes on self-actualization as an ultimate solution, the creation of an industrial environment in which every individual can attain the aspired satisfaction and fulfilment dictated by his current needs, but the translation of such an objective to tangible formulae for organization design continues to elude us.

THE PROBLEM OF GOAL INTEGRATION

McGregor lays emphasis on the need for integration between individual and organizational objectives, and he sees "genuine potential for a linkage of self-actualization with organizational goals" [2, p. 77], although it is not clear how such a linkage could be established. "Management's purpose is to influence behaviour toward the achievement of organizational objectives" [1, p. 30], and "the central principle which derives from Theory Y is that of integration: the creation of conditions such that the members of the organization can achieve their own goals best by directing their efforts towards the success of the enterprise" [1, p. 49], but the implicit assumption is that conditions can in fact be created where the two are compatible. What if they are not? What if a conflict between the two does exist or if the attainment of objectives and self-actualization for one group of employees in the enterprise can be achieved at the expense of another group? We are clearly a long way from providing convincing and tangible answers to these problems.

And so, for the benefit of those who are still debating with some vehemence the rights and wrongs of the two alternative theories, let me end with a quotation from McGregor's final words in his last book:

"The purpose of this volume is not to entice management to choose sides over Theory X or Theory Y. It is rather to encourage the realization that theory is important, to urge management to examine its assumptions and make them explicit. In doing so it will open a door to the future. The possible result could be developments during the next few decades with respect to the human side of enterprise comparable to those that have occurred in technology during the past half century.

"And, if we can learn how to realize the potential for collaboration inherent in the human resources of industry, we will provide a model for governments and nations which mankind sorely needs." [2, p. 46.]

REFERENCES

1. McGregor, D. (1960) *The Human Side of Enterprise,* McGraw-Hill.
2. McGregor, D. (1967) *The Professional Manager,* McGraw-Hill.

CHAPTER 4

Are You a 9 – 9 Man?

Many authors have written extensively about managerial styles. Likert, for example, presented what he calls "four systems of management": System 1—exploitive authoritative, System 2—benevolent authoritative, System 3—consultative, System 4—participative, McGregor's books dwell on Theory X and Theory Y as two extreme philosophies that determine managerial behaviour and style;[1] Herzberg and Mausner, and others, discuss reward systems and the way they affect, or should affect, such behaviour.

In all these writings on managerial style attempts are made to highlight contrasting approaches—the authoritarian versus the consultative; the paternalistic versus the communal; the mechanistic versus the human; the unitarist versus the pluralist. And while many authors take a very partisan stance, condemning one style and applauding the other, some are more cautious in their prescriptions of universal recipes for management to follow and are content to speculate on the possible consequences of adopting or changing a given style, leaving the reader to decide on his own attitudes and preferences in this matter.

Perhaps none of the writings on managerial style has had as far reaching an impact as the Grid method of Blake and Mouton [1], which I shall now explore in some detail. Extensive Grid Seminars and Grid OD (Organization Development) programmes in many industrial companies, sometimes extending over substantial time periods, have made the Grid familiar to many consultants and managers concerned with organizational change. The Grid is provided by Blake and Mouton as a vehicle for describing a variety of managerial styles and—in their view—to help identify the characteristics needed for corporate excellence. Indeed, their book is entitled *Corporate*

---

[1] See Chapter 3.

39

Excellence through Grid Organization Development, and it proceeds to
specify in great detail six phases in their proposed OD programme, even
the amount of time to be spent on every activity in the Grid Seminar,
the instructional material involved, the role of the OD co-ordinator, and the
assessment of progress. It is their contention that "Grid Organization is an
approach to achieving an ideal of corporate excellence to strive toward and
to perfecting a sound system of management which can convert striving
into execution" [1, p. 2].

Now the first question that is bound to be asked is what is meant by corporate excellence. And Blake and Mouton answer this question with the
following definition: "An excellent corporation is able to achieve and sustain an outstandingly high return on investment over long periods of time.
Its managers have learnt how to identify and create new opportunities while
meeting present responsibilities. . . . The excellent corporation increasingly
strives to increase the competence of its managers to manage and its employees to produce. . . . The concept of synergy is understood and exploited."
And so on [1, p. 2]. This string of attractive sentiments, expressing highly
desirable aspirations, cannot fail to exact the warm approval of any manager, although the degree to which such aspirations and subsequent achievements can be quantified in an objective and persuasive way remains very
much in doubt.[2]

But let us assume for a moment that a picture of corporate excellence
can be painted, however vague and amorphous. It is then natural to explore
the reasons for a given enterprise not achieving it, and Blake and Mouton
discuss at some length various "barriers to corporate effectiveness", singling
out shortcomings in communication and planning and listing symptoms
which are common and are readily recognizable in many organizations. They
then embark on a detailed exposition of their Grid OD as a means of identifying the deficiencies and overcoming the problems of implementing change.

The Grid is in fact a two-dimensional representation of a manager's concern, attitude, or behaviour in relation to "production" and "people". The
first (horizontal) dimension is his concern for production (interpreted widely
as task-orientation, not confined to the production function), with a scale of
1 (low concern) to 9 (high concern). And since people have to work with or

[2] See Chapter 15.

through people, the second (vertical) dimension denotes the manager's concern in that respect, again with a scale of 1 (low) to 9 (high). Thus, the Grid is a 9 x 9 matrix, each cell representing a set of combinations of values on the two scales.

Of the eighty-one cells in the Grid five are singled out for special discussion [1, p. 15]: the man typified as 1 - 1 exerts the "minimum effort to get required work done" that will still retain his membership of the organization; the 9 - 1 man is primarily concerned with "efficiency in operation results", the human element interfering with those "to a minimum degree", the 1 - 9 man's "thoughtful attention to needs of people for satisfying relationships leads to a comfortable friendly organization atmosphere and work tempo"; the fourth is the 5 - 5 man, who believes that "adequate organization performance is possible through balancing the necessity to get out work with maintaining morale of people at a satisfactory level"; finally, the *nonplus-ultra* is the 9 - 9 man, whose credo is that "work accomplishment is from committed people; interdependence through a 'common stake' in organization purpose leads to relationships of trust and respect". And superimposed on this Grid as a third dimension, "the thickness or depth of a man's theory" [1, p. 27]: a "deep 9 - 9 man will persist in searching for solutions to problems in a 9 - 9 way, whereas a "shallow 9 - 9" man will abandon that approach as soon as difficulties arise.

If you are baffled by the definition of the 9 - 9 man and wonder what it really means, do not despair; Blake and Mouton proceed to describe the attributes that a 9 - 9 man should develop, and the way that he would avoid and manage conflict. The approach is to use empirical data in the decision-making process ("faith is out, facts are in"). If managers are committed to study, analysis, and logic, if "facts, not personalities, are the source of power and determine the course of action", if an attempt is made to get to the cause of barriers when they are encountered—then the "9 - 9 theory" is fully vindicated. Whether it is realistic to hope that facts and logic can eliminate disparities between systems of value judgement, power struggle, and political manoeuvring, is another matter.

Now, to be fair, Blake and Mouton are careful not to prescribe the 9 - 9 theory as the path to corporate excellence, but they certainly come very close to it. They start with the premise that "If a corporation is to achieve excellence, it is important that every man in the organization has a deep personal understanding as well as a shared commitment to a model of an ideal manager and an ideal corporate culture. The two are inseparable" [1, pp. 27 - 29]. This is a strongly worded and uncompromising premise, the justification for which is far from clear, and many will read into it an endorsement of the dedicated organization man, a "cog in the wheel" by consent (even conviction). But if by some twist of logic it does not follow that the ideal prototype manager (endorsed by "every man in the organization") is an organization man, and if we were to accept that such a single prototype is compatible with—nay, essential for—corporate excellence, which type should it be?

Blake and Mouton argue that "the Grid alternatives provide a rich variety of possibilities from which the surest path to excellence can be selected", and state that having studied the Grid for a week most organization members conclude that the 9 - 9 theory is best, and that a strong preference for 9 - 9 remains in these organizations subsequently. As a typical example, the views are quoted of managers in one company subjected to Grid OD, listing many appealing virtues in a "9 - 9 Work Culture", such as: having a forthright and unobstructed communication with bosses and subordinates, full commitment to organization objectives, searching and finding valid solutions to problems, experimenting with innovative and creative solutions, accepting nothing short of excellent results, and so on.

One might speculate that following a group induction to the Grid prototypes, and the inevitable affinity between this list of virtues and the definition of the 9 - 9 man, it would be a very strong-willed person who could withstand corporate and group pressure to disassociate himself from such a paragon. It would be very surprising indeed if faced with a selection from the five major types in the Grid, most people did not single out the 9 - 9 man as their first choice and the 1 - 1 man as their last. For it is the manner in which the alternatives are presented that may well determine such a choice. To put it crudely, if you offer an individual the choice between prize A or prize B or prize A plus B, would you be astonished if he prefers the third? When one alternative clearly dominates another, a choice between them is not real. A meaningful choice can only exist when trade-offs are patently involved, for example in having to state a preference between 1 - 9, 5 - 5, and 9 - 1.

There is another premise implied by Blake and Mouton which cannot remain unchallenged, namely that because most inductees of the Grid Seminar choose 9 - 9, it is necessarily the best path to corporate excellence. Hard empirical evidence is required to substantiate such a claim, and the subjective attitude of people extracted under very subjective conditions can hardly be regarded as evidence for this purpose. Surely examples can be quoted of outstanding managers, who have led their organizations to great achievements and who would not be regarded by their colleagues or subordinates as anything like resembling 9 - 9 types.

There is yet another proposition in the Grid OD method which raises serious doubts, namely that the 9 - 9 man is a commonly attainable type. Since it incorporates the maximum achievement on two counts—in production and in dealing with people—it would naturally seem attractive, but is it feasible? To say that "the 9 - 9 theory is a synergistic theory of behavior", fusing together concern for both dimensions, has implications—but, alas, no proof—of feasibility. This is not to say that 9 - 9 men do not exist, but that many can be found or created is doubtful.

Since one of the implied assumptions of Grid OD is that people can be converted in appreciable numbers from one type to another, we need to examine the basis for such a premise. The attributes that characterize a man in the Grid are the results of his background, upbringing, personality, and the forces in the internal and external environments. A multitude of pressures, relationships, aspirations, and parameters of his personal identity combine to mould his behaviour. No doubt Grid OD can contribute to change the company environment and prevailing attitudes, to make an individual aware of his shortcomings (as seen by him and acknowledged by others), and to help him make certain adjustments. But to what extent such a programme can achieve a revolutionary change in stance is less clear.

These objections, and others only briefly alluded to, raise many questions about the validity of the basic propositions of the Grid OD programme and the manner of its implementation. In view of what appears to be rather shaky theoretical foundations, one must ponder on what it is that has made Grid OD so popular in recent years; there is no denying that it has enjoyed acclaim from many quarters, and surely a product cannot be bad—its innovators might argue—if it is in great demand.

The answer lies, in my view, not in the product but in the process, not in what it is, but in what it does. Grid OD, with its almost engaging naivety and the mechanistic mentality of a "snakes and ladders" game, may be regarded simply as a means for stirring the pot; it poses problems to people, it challenges, cajoles, even threatens them; it gathers people together, it presents them with tasks, it underlines relentlessly the need for communication and ⋅ co-operation. And stirring the pot is important; organizations become too static, too obdurate, too ossified, when there is no serious and imminent threat from the outside. Any effective way of challenging this complacency (provided it is not done too often or irresponsibly is bound to be beneficial to the organization, even to its members.

Now, Grid OD may well be an effective way of stirring the pot, but the implications of its basic assumptions are too serious for us to brush aside the possible negative side-effects resulting from its pressures on individuals and on the organization to conform. If the objective of the exercise is to achieve organizational change, let us remember that there are other, perhaps less pretentious, techniques that can be employed: changes in organization design, rotation of personnel, changes in procedures, brainstorming sessions, task forces for special purposes, post mortems—all these can be just as challenging, just as penetrating, just as effective.

REFERENCE

1. Blake, R. R., and Mouton, J. S. (1968) *Corporate Excellence through Grid Organization Development*, Gulf, Texas.

CHAPTER 5

The Myth of Self-Actualization

> I have come to the conclusion that
> my subjective account of my own
> motivation is largely mythical on
> almost all occasions. I don't know
> why I do things. (J. B. S. Haldane)

One of the most-favoured pastimes of industrial sociologists over the last
three decades has been the debunking of Taylorism. "Scientific management", which Taylor fervently advocated at the beginning of the century,
was founded on the belief that work can be the subject of systematic observation and analysis, and in consequence it can be so organized as to make
the best use of human resources in the enterprise. "The principal object of
management should be to secure the maximum prosperity for the employer,
coupled with the maximum prosperity of each employee" [5]. In Taylor's
view, the blatant inefficiencies found in industrial operations stem, on the
one hand, from "systematic soldiering" by workers (a graphic description of
their deliberate action to restrict their output) resulting from their sincere
though misguided belief that increased output must lead to increased unemployment (a belief which he felt was amply justified by their experience),
and on the other hand from ineffective management in failing to organize the
work properly and to provide the necessary incentive. What workers want
above all, he argued, is high wages, and what employers wish to achieve is
minimum unit costs; the two objectives can be made compatible by the following means: a clear specification of the tasks that need to be performed, a
proper selection of workers for these tasks, a training scheme to ensure that

each worker can attain the highest degree of effectiveness in performing the task allocated to him, a piece-rate system to provide a financial reward to the worker for increased output, and responsible behaviour by management not to cut rates when output rises. The basic tenet of Taylor is that men have different capabilities, and while one may be "first-class" at performing one job, he may be less suitable for another. It is the duty of management, he contended, to identify men with potential for each job and to train them to become "first-class" men to perform "the highest, most interesting and most profitable class of work", thereby meeting the needs of the enterprise and the aspirations of the workers at the same time.

Pressed as to what he meant by "first-class" men, Taylor resorted to an illustration involving a stable of, say, 300 or 400 horses. In such a stable "you will have a certain number of horses which are intended especially for hauling coal wagons; you will have a certain number of other horses intended especially to haul grocery wagons; you will have a certain number of trotting horses; a certain number of saddle horses—of pleasure horses, and of ponies" [5, testimony, pp. 172 - 3]; similarly, heavily built men are suited to do heavy work, at which they could be "first-class", but they may be unsuited to do light work, for which they would then be "second-class". If they possess the appropriate physique for a given job but are unable or obstinately refuse to learn how to perform it, then they too would be regarded by Taylor as "second-class" men. Such men must be found tasks at which they will become "first-class", or else they have no place in Taylor's scheme. "Scientific management has no place for a bird that can sing and won't sing", he said in 1912 in his testimony before the Special House Committee of the US House of Representatives, and added more specifically: "No man who can work and won't work has any place under scientific management." He further asserted that "there is no one kind of work that suits all types of men" and those who are willing to work must have some jobs for which they will be so suited as to become "first-class" in their execution.

One can understand the wrath that Taylor's ideas have generated. He was accused of total disregard of human values. It was argued that Taylor's training as an engineer naturally led him to regard the factory purely as a physical system, with deterministic and predictable outcomes for given levels of inputs and stimuli. Such a mechanistic view of the work environment is based on the assumption that the workers have an overwhelming and honest desire to maximize their financial rewards, so that an appropriate carrot system can be devised to encourage them to work harder and to produce more. To compare a man to an animal, to regard him as no different from a well-oiled machine set up to perform tasks in a rigidly prescribed manner (which is what training in Taylor's scheme is all about) and to expect him to react predictably to wage incentives—all this is anathema to those who seek to understand man's motivation and to advance his social (and not only physical) welfare.

Taylor-baiting is all the more understandable in the light of post-Taylor developments in work-design in industry. His postulate that people's aptitudes vary has led to ever-increasing specialization, where work is divided into well-defined components and allotted to specially designed work stations and where men perform limited tasks, often of short cycle durations. Assisted by time and motion study, jigs and fixtures, work place layout design, and accelerated rates of mechanization, mass production has become totally dependent on flow-line manufacture, characterized by the men on the conveyor belt, where the main problem concerning the industrial engineer is that of line balancing to smooth variations in cycle times of sequential tasks on the line, and where monotony of work is an essential element in the attainment of high line efficiency. The process of de-humanizing work has thereby become quite inevitable; not only has division of work led to a diminution of the range of duties performed by the individual worker, but the skill required for the task has similarly declined. Thus, specialization (which we often regard as synonymous with division of work) resulted in the need for fewer and fewer specialists, in a de-skilling process, in monotony and boredom, at least for those concerned with the manning of the production line. Instead of industry selecting men with potential and training them to become "first-class" men, as Taylor envisaged, it allows its sequential work tasks to become so interdependent and therefore so simplified and impersonalized, that almost anyone can be made to undertake them; indeed, the training required for the purpose is often quite minimal. Gone is the concept of the "first-class" man; the system has made him redundant. And as a consequence the basic notion of Taylor that every worker should be employed to the full use of his capabilities has gone by the board. Simple mechanical tasks of short cycle times are not conducive to exploiting man's full potential; the monotony and pressure of work on the production line, paced as it almost

invariably is by the conveyor belt, is not sufficiently compensated by the
relatively high financial rewards, and frustration and alienation often ensue.

It would be unfair to lay the blame for the industrial unrest during the
last half a century on Taylorism; his philosophy and ideas on the organization of work need to be judged against the industrial environment at the
beginning of the century, and not against present-day conditions. Leavitt is
one of the few who recognizes this point when he says [3, p. 544] : "In so
eagerly demolishing Taylorism we may have thrown out some useful parts
of the baby with the bath water. We may even be repeating some of the mis-
takes of Taylorism that we have taken such pains to point out." And in the
context of the industrial problems facing Taylor at the time, he had some
sound advice to give, coupled with genuine concern for the prosperity and
welfare of the workers. The fact that he was such an ardent advocate of the
piece-rate system, stemming from his conviction of the overriding importance to the worker of financial rewards, should be applauded and not condemned. We must bear in mind the low standard of living of industrial workers and the high degree of authoritarian control exercised in factories at the
beginning of the century to appreciate that Taylor's methods gave real opportunities for workers to increase their earnings substantially and urged management to improve production facilities. That fifty years after Taylor we have
begun to realize the shortcomings of the piece-rate system—its failure to stop
"systematic soldiering", its inequities, and the lasting damage it inflicted on
the authority and responsibilities of middle management in industry—is not
Taylor's fault (indeed, he was at pains to point out that piece-rate schemes on
their own had done nothing to abate the practice of soldiering); it is the fault
of the intervening generations who allowed the system to become increasingly outmoded and who failed to adapt it. Taylor would certainly not have
obdurately clung to the principles he enunciated in 1911 had he lived through
the experiences of industrial society of the last few decades.

And so, with the increasing realization that the proposition of "maximum
prosperity for the employer coupled with the maximum prosperity of each
employee" does not hold and that wage incentive schemes have a limited success, observers of the industrial scene turned their attention to the question
of motivation. What makes people work? What would make them work harder? How can labour productivity be increased? What causes alienation, rebel-
lion, and industrial strife? Can the interests of the employer and the interests

of the employee be brought together, or should we accept that the conflict between them is inherent in their different roles and aspirations, in which case should we institutionalize the process of conflict resolution and even resort to structured conflict to improve industrial performance?

It is therefore not surprising that writers in the field began to question the fundamental concept of *economic man*—namely that man's behaviour is largely if not solely dictated by economic considerations—and began to explore various facets of *emotional man*. These ideas were aptly summarized by Leavitt [3, pp. 3 - 4] :

1. "People exhibit a wide variety of needs, drives, or motives, ranging from very basic physical needs, through ego and security needs, to social and achievement needs."
2. "Within limits, people do tend to concentrate their energies on only a few of their needs at a time. The others are put aside, either because they are sated or because they are too far off to be of immediate operational value."
3. "People seldom seek complete satisfaction of their needs. They tend to try for goals which are adequate or good enough, rather than the best of all possible goals."
4. "Feelings of conflict result either when the goals are set higher than one's achievement potential or when a person perceives his several needs to be inconsistent. These feelings of conflict in turn tend to cause off-beat behavior, like withdrawal from a situation or 'irrational' hostility."

The notion of a variety of motivations was proposed in some detail by Maslow [4] in his widely quoted hierarchy of needs. Man has, he argues, certain physiological needs, starting perhaps with those relating to hunger, thirst, intake of certain chemicals, sex, and so on, ranging over a wide spectrum. "It is quite true that man lives by bread alone—when there is no bread. But what happens to man's desires when there *is* plenty of bread and when his belly is chronically filled? *At once other (and higher) needs emerge* and these, rather than physiological hungers, dominate the organism. And when these in turn are satisfied, again new (and still higher) needs emerge and so on. This is what we mean by saying that the basic human needs are organized into a hierarchy of relative prepotency" [4, p. 9] .

Thus, Maslow suggests that the spectrum of man's physiological needs is indeed a wide one, and beyond them there are four further sets of needs: needs for safety and security, needs for love and affection, needs for achievement and esteem, and finally, to be ultimately happy, man has a need for *self-actualization,* the supreme goal. "What a man *can* be, he *must* be. This need we may call self-actualization. . . . It refers to the desire for self-fulfilment, namely for one to become actualized in what one is potentially. This tendency might be phrased as the desire to become more and more what one is, to become everything that one is capable of becoming" [4, p. 16]. Maslow argues that "most of the people with whom we have worked have seemed to have these basic needs in about the order that has been indicated", but he is flexible enough to admit that there are exceptions of those who have their priorities arranged differently, those whose level of aspiration has been permanently deadened, or those with "psychopathic personality"; but these exceptions do not deviate Maslow from his general theme that "man is a perpetually wanting animal", that he has at least five sets of goals (called the *basic needs*) arranged as a hierarchy of prepotency, that the prepotent need at any time dominates man's consciousness, and when it is satisfied a new "higher" need emerges, and that self-actualization represents the ultimate in human aspiration.

The theme is followed up by many writers (see, for example, [1]). Looking at the problem from another angle, Herzberg proposes his motivation - hygiene theory as a means of analysing job satisfaction. He is sceptical of what he believes has developed as a myth among management theorists, namely that if management ensures that the worker is paid, is well treated, and is comfortable, it should then expect to reap all the benefits from the worker's motivational desires. He argues [2] that there are five factors that determine job satisfaction: achievement, recognition, work itself, responsibility, and advancement—these are the motivators which arise from "a need for growth or self-actualization". And similarly there are five major dissatisfiers: company policy and administration, supervision, salary, interpersonnel relations, and working conditions—these he terms the hygiene factors. He argues that the set of motivators and the set of dissatisfiers reflect "a two-dimensional need structure: one need for the avoidance of unpleasantness and a parallel need system for personal growth", that in his empirical study "the factors involved in producing job satisfaction were *separate* and *distinct* from the factors that led to job dissatisfaction", and he concludes that the two sets are "not the obverse of each other" [2, pp. 75 - 76]. He argues that by recognizing the work-hygiene needs and the motivational needs, management can identify the factors that will lead to job satisfaction and provide opportunities for self-realization: "the child will never, never learn to ride the bicycle—unless he is given a bicycle, similarly creativity requires that a man is given a potentially creative task to do" [2, p. 75]. There is here the clear implication that man's job should be so designed as to make full use of his potential and to meet his needs both in terms of physical as well as spiritual aspirations.

Thus, we have come full circle. Was it not Taylor who said that man should perform "the highest, most interesting and most profitable class of work"? Was it not he who argued that—properly motivated—the workers will respond positively and bring about the desired prosperity both to them and to the enterprise in which they work? Take away his prime preoccupation with financial rewards and his faith in what he regarded as properly designed piece-rate systems and you have a message not dissimilar to the one proposed by the Maslow school: man has certain needs and expectations, he also has certain capabilities and potential; meet his needs, give him an opportunity to use his potential, to be "first-class" at his job, and you have a satisfied man performing well for the good of all.

This is obviously a gross oversimplification. There is a very fundamental difference between Taylorism and Maslowism in their perception of needs and motivation. For one thing, Taylor sees incentives based entirely on the concept of economic man, whereas Maslow argues that prepotency of hierarchical needs requires a dynamic - evolving motivational scheme, not a static one based on a single need. For another, Maslow envisages self-actualization as the ultimate goal for all, whereas Taylor urged us to recognize that people vary in their aptitudes and capabilities, and hence in their suitability to undertake various tasks. Most important of all, Taylorism and Maslowism diverge in their conclusions on job organization: in Taylor's scheme division of work, selection, and training to perform given jobs are paramount; the Maslow school would argue for job enlargement and a constant reappraisal of individual job specification to promote job satisfaction.

But the basic problem remains: How do you reconcile the needs of the individual with the needs of the organization as well as the needs of other individuals? What evidence do we have to suggest that it is always feasible for people to develop to their full potential? Ignoring for the moment the fact that Taylor's principle of division of work has led to the lowering of the level of skill required for many jobs in manufacturing industry and therefore to the negation of the concept of the elitist "first-class" men for these jobs, one must ask whether the need of society for various jobs exactly equates the distribution of "first-class" men in society. And this is precisely what the Chairman of the Special House Committee, Mr. W. B. Wilson, did ask: "How does scientific management propose to take care of men who are not 'first-class' in any particular line of work?", to which the exasperated Taylor retorted "I give up" and then reiterated his view that every man, provided he is willing to work, is "first-class" at something and there is therefore no question of having to deal with men who are not "first class". But the Chairman persisted: "Do you mean to tell the committee that society is so balanced that it just provides the proper number of individuals who are well fitted to a particular line of work to furnish society with the products of that line of work?" [5, testimony, p. 176].

Wilson's principle of imbalance (as we may call it) equally applies to Maslow's self-actualization. "A musician must make music, an artist must paint, a poet must write, if he is to be ultimately happy. What a man *can* be, he *must* be." But if a particular individual can be a musician and the enterprise that he works for has no need for a musician, or already employs as many musicians as it needs, how can that individual become self-actualized in that environment? Should we expect the enterprise to employ him as a musician nonetheless? And if the enterprise continues to accommodate similar needs, will it survive? Or should the individual leave, in which case how can we be sure that his needs can be met in full elsewhere?

This is not to deny that job enlargement and job enrichment are possible in many work situations, but it would be naive to regard them as a panacea or even to think that they can be universally applied without ill effects. It often transpires that job enlargement and added responsibility for individual A can be achieved only by job contraction for individual B, or at least the denial of job enlargement for B as well. We are reminded here by the proposition, often stated, that the relentless pursuit of total individual freedom cannot be condoned without regard to its effects on society, and that the attainment of greater freedom of action for one man may well mean the denial of some freedom of action to others. I am not arguing that the "fixed cake" for the work system always holds, namely that the total tasks and responsibilities in a given work environment remains constant irrespective of how they are allocated among departments and individuals. Some room for manoeuvre for job definition must exist, but jobs are not infinitely adjustable, and when job enlargement is embarked upon a point must soon be reached when either jobs substantially overlap, resulting in gross misuse of resources, or tasks are not adequately manned. And particularly on the last point: What do you do when certain tasks are shunned by all, when in a production department everyone wants to be foreman and no one wants to be an operator, or when in an office everyone wants to manage and no one wants to type? It is no use saying that the job can be so organized that an individual can be both foreman and operator, or both office manager and typist; someone has to do the manual, mundane, and routine tasks: if they are to be performed solely by some, as suggested by Taylor, how can they become self-actualized in the Maslow sense, and if they are to be spread amongst the many, how can everyone be satisfied with the outcome?

Inherent in the philosophy of self-actualization is that it represents the ultimate in man's needs. But if "man is a wanting animal" as suggested by Maslow (a maxim that observers of the human condition are bound to endorse), and if new needs emerge when old ones are fulfilled, how can there be an ultimate state which does not generate new desires? The answer lies in the proposition that self-actualization is a manifestation of man's satisfaction derived from creative work. A writer does not look for "job enlargement"; he looks for new stimuli and new ideas that will ensure that he continues to write, and his creative drive is the source of his self-fulfilment. Such a writer may be said to be self-actualized. But herein lies the problem of self-actualization when we turn to the world of industry and business. In the first instance, most of the work involved is not creative in the sense in which writers, sculptors, or inventors regard creative work, so that any one advocating self-actualization for all simply disregards the realities of life. Secondly, and this is perhaps even more important, what motivates many people in social systems beyond their basic needs is their desire for added responsibility, for power and authority, and you cannot run an enterprise in which everyone acts as the chief executive.

Self-actualization for all is a myth. It is doubtful whether it has any meaning as the ultimate goal for every individual, and whether such ultimate goals of spiritual well-being—even if they do exist—are identical for different people. But in the main, Taylorism and Maslowism strive to self-fulfilment through the use of man to his full potential and capabilities; neither tell us how this El Dorado is to be found.

REFERENCES

1. Bindra, D., and Stewart, J. (eds., 1966) *Motivation,* Penguin Books.
2. Herzberg, F. (1968) *Work and the Nature of Man,* Staples Press.
3. Leavitt, H. J., and Pondy, L. R. (eds., 1964) *Readings in Managerial Psychology* University of Chicago Press.
4. Maslow, A. H. (1954) *Motivation and Personality,* Harper & Bros.
5. Taylor, F. W. (1911; reprinted 1947) *Scientific Management (incorporating: Shop Management, The Principles of Scientific Management, and Testimony before the Special House Committee),* Harper & Bros.

CHAPTER 6

On the Corporate Ethos

"The prime purpose of an enterprise is to maximize the wealth of its shareholders." This is a maxim that has been widely held and cherished for many years. The very thought that it could possibly be questioned has been considered by many as nothing short of sheer heresy.

And yet there is clearly now a growing concern about the relationships, duties, and responsibilities of an industrial enterprise with and towards society as a whole, and the notion that the enterprise has allegiance only to its shareholders is under challenge. A typical, and by no means rare, expression of this concern was made by Sir Frederick Catherwood when he said:

"If we make losses, we go out of business; if our profits are too low, we cannot expand and improve our products. So we must care for the interests of the owners. But if we do not care for the interests of the customer, he will buy elsewhere. If we do not care for the interests of the workers, they will work elsewhere. If we do not pay our creditors in time, our suppliers will disappear. If we harm the public, government will stop us. It is not the business of the professional manager to look after the owners to the exclusion of customers, workers, creditors and the public, but to reconcile all these interests." [1]

Strictly, there is nothing very revolutionary in these sentiments. Even those who staunchly support the thesis that the directors of a company are the legal and moral custodians of the shareholders cannot deny the proposition that suppliers and workers must be paid, and that capital expenditure is essential to safeguard the long-term interests of the company.

Some may interpret Catherwood, and those who echo his pronouncements, as a plea for the justification of the profit motive, a kind of apologia to those who criticize the proposition that the sole object of an enterprise is to make profit, let alone maximize it.

Flew [2] rejects the suggestion that the profit motive provides the only reason for a product being produced and sold, since motives are notoriously mixed. "That this is one of his [the manufacturer's] motives by no means precludes that he has other motives also. A man may invest his capital in a bassoon factory because he wants a profitable investment; and because he wants to popularise bassoon-playing; and because he wants to infuriate his unmusical aunt." Accepting, therefore, the proposition that profit is not the *only* motive, it is still possible to argue—as Catherwood has done so eloquently—that in the absence of subsidies the profit element is necessary in order to keep the business going. Unless there is profit it is not possible to invest in plant and machinery, to expand, to diversify, or to engage in any new activities that may be thought appropriate for the firm, other than maintenance of the status quo that could lead to decline and eventual extinction; nor is it possible to compensate shareholders adequately (if at all) for their investment, and this can only discourage any future investors from coming forward.

These arguments are forceful enough and they cannot be brushed aside by the retort that "it all depends on what profit means", and that if payments to shareholders and provision for capital expenditure are to be counted as costs and not included in the residual element which we now call "profit", then all would be well, since people would be better informed about the needs of the enterprise and would see no reason to attack legitimate expenditure. Alas, the problem would still remain and would focus instead on the level of reserves (which include future capital expenditure and provisions for bad debts and unfavourable trading), on the amount to be paid to shareholders (who are always regarded as a category apart from the lenders), and on whatever residue remains beyond these items.

As Flew remarks, "that it is essentially scandalous to make a profit— and hence, presumably, also scandalous to wish to do so—is an idea both as old as the classical Greek philosophers and as topical as tomorrow's party political broadcasts." These ideas harp remorselessly on the theme that profit represents some kind of exploitation, either of the customer or the workforce or both. What is needed, we are told, is the development of what some people call a "non-exploitive ethic".

But exploitation is an emotive term. It has the connotation of someone being short-changed by having to give goods or services against his will. It presupposes a zero-sum game, in which the benefits to two players add up to zero, so that one can only win if the other loses, whereas in a free market this is not the case. Unless he is faced with a monopoly, the customer has a choice whether to buy or not. The fact that he is prepared to part with his money to acquire a given product means that he is at least indifferent as to whether the sum of money in question or the product has a greater value to him, and presumably he prefers the product to the money if he is actively seeking to make the exchange. Similarly, the manufacturer has a choice to keep the product or to sell at a price, and his preference is to have the money. The transaction between the seller and buyer involves no coercion; both want the exchange of money and goods to take place, each side sees a benefit to himself. The same argument applies to the payment for and use of labour, which in this context is no different from other commodities. In a free society, where the game is dependent on the willingness of the players to play, it must be concluded that the manufacture and distribution of a product is a non-zero-sum game, where all the participants stand to gain from it. It is, of course, possible in a non-zero-sum game for one player to get a disproportionate amount of the spoils, at least as seen by the other players involved. For example, if the price for a given product is raised and if the customer is still prepared to pay for it, the resultant benefit to the manufacturer would increase, while the benefit to customer would decrease (although he would still have a positive payoff, otherwise he would not buy). The charge of exploitation in such a case is based on the proposition that the manufacturer takes something away from the customer, not actually but notionally, and causes a "fair" return to the customer to decrease. What is or is not fair in the resolution of non-zero-sum games is a matter for debate, and this is precisely what the argument on profit is all about.

Perhaps the major facets of this discussion could be better examined with reference to two major questions that closely interact. The first is "How much profit should an enterprise aim to achieve?", and the second "How should the profit be distributed?"

HOW MUCH PROFIT?

There are two philosophies on this question. The first advocates *profit maximization* and argues that in any industrial or commercial activity it is legitimate to strive for the maximum achievable surplus for a given level of resources. In this sense an excessive profit margin is only excessive when it adversely affects demand to the extent that the rate of return on the resources employed begins to suffer.

This approach has several almost inevitable consequences: an incentive to minimize the cost of production, a temptation to increase prices whenever possible, a disregard for the environment and for the implications of the company's actions on the outside world inasmuch as these effects are not detrimental to the rate of return.

The philosophy of the profit maximizer is embedded in his conviction that "the business of business is business". Not for him are the niceties of human relations or concern for the customers or the environment for its own sake. For him such concern can only be justified if it has a positive contribution to profit performance. It is not the responsibility of business, he argues, to look after public amenities, to improve or preserve the environment, to contribute to charities or to the arts; all these laudable causes, in his view, are the responsibilities of local and national government, and business enterprises should not undertake functions outside their prime purpose, which is to engage in whatever business they were set up to do and to make money. The major contribution of business in this respect comes from the payment of taxes—both by corporations and their employees— and it is up to the government to decide how these taxes should be used and what the priorities for public expenditure should be. This is, after all, what government is for, and business has neither the facility nor the mandate to encroach on the government's domain. Thus, if there is anything in the realm of social behaviour that the government feels should become part of the code of conduct by business—constraints on the production of harmful products, control of air or water pollution, abatement of excessive noise or fumes, avoiding damage to the countryside, and so on—then government should legislate as appropriate, and business would obey the law accordingly.

This simple-minded logic is criticized by the adherents of the second philosophy that a business enterprise does and should have a responsibility to the community, that it is sufficient to have an *adequate level of profit* (or an *acceptable rate of return on investment*). Below this level the performance of the enterprise would be regarded as unsatisfactory, but no attempt should be made to end up with an unduly large surplus, "to squeeze the last drop out of the system", so to speak. This philosophy is based on the proposition that an adequate return is necessary to keep the system going, but it is not its sole objective. Indeed, in this context profit (or return) becomes a constraint, one amongst many that the enterprise needs to observe. Other constraints may involve minimum quality norms, self-imposed safety and operational standards, an upper limit to the utilization of machinery or plant, minimum treatment procedures of waste materials, and so on. Some of these constraints may be more important or more demanding than others, but profit is not regarded as the overriding criterion.

It may be argued that the two philosophies are not that different, since in the case of profit maximization there are always certain constraints in operation, so that once the constraints are observed it is perfectly legitimate to maximize the possible outcome in profit terms. But the basic difference between maximum profit and adequate profit is that the former is largely concerned with externally imposed constraints and is prepared to tolerate self-imposed constraints only on operational grounds, whereas the latter is amenable to the introduction of ethical considerations, which tend to be ignored when actions leading to profit maximization so demand.

The maxim of adequate profit is becoming more widely acceptable, and to some extent it does abate the virulent assault on the profit motive, but the question "How much profit?" still remains. What is regarded by some as adequate profit may be seen by others as excessive. There is no way of specifying absolute standards that would be acceptable to all. In arriving at a value for adequate profit or return, the management of the enterprise needs to be mindful of public reaction, of expectations of customers, of alternative forms of investment, and of the performance and behaviour of competitors.

HOW TO DISTRIBUTE PROFIT?

But perhaps what matters more about profit is what you do with it once you have it. Table 6.1 shows how profit can be distributed. First, a distinction needs to be made between the short term and the long term. The former relates to immediate benefits that can be obtained, the latter to capital investment.

TABLE 6.1. *Distribution of profit*

| | TOTAL SURPLUS | |
DISTRIBUTION TO	SHORT TERM Immediate benefits	LONG TERM Capital investment
Shareholders	Dividends	Invest in new plant
Employees	Profit sharing	Improve working environment
Customers	Price reduction	Improve products
Society	Donations	Improve general environment

Table 6.1 identifies four beneficiaries: shareholders, employees, customers, and society. In the short term shareholders benefit through dividends, but they also have (assuming they intend to continue as shareholders) an interest in capital expenditure in new plant and machinery, in research and development, in diversification, in acquisitions of new companies and facilities—if such an expenditure is likely to keep the performance of the enterprise at a high level, or improve it.

The short-term benefits to employees—apart from wages and salaries—is in the form of bonuses or profit sharing. In the long term they have a common interest with the shareholders in the continued prosperity of the enterprise, and are therefore concerned with capital expenditure on plant, but they also have an interest in the improvement of the physical working environment, in the provision of various "non-productive" facilities, in longer holidays, and in training and educational opportunities.

Customers can gain in the short term through price reductions, while capital expenditure can lead to the improvement of the company's products, resulting in long-term benefits to the customers.

And, finally, society can benefit if the company is generous enough to make donations to deserving causes (such as academic or social institutions), or to take action to improve local or national amenities. Some of these actions have a short term effect, others—involving capital expenditure—are of a more lasting nature.

Few companies explicitly plan their profit distribution in this way. Immediate dividends to shareholders are usually of prime concern, not only because of the sense of duty that managements feel to their shareholders, but also because of the possible effect on share price and retribution from dissatisfied shareholders. The interests of the beneficiaries in Table 6.1 are quite diverse, and sometimes in direct conflict, and because of the immediate power that shareholders can exercise—at least in theory—at annual general meetings, it is not surprising that their interest tends to dominate. But the power of the other beneficiaries is on the increase, as various recent cases clearly demonstrate, and it is against the total picture of profit distribution—as suggested in Table 6.1—that the behaviour of an enterprise will have to be judged. The debate between the profit maximizer and the profit satisfier is by no means over, and a conscious and systematic re-appraisal of the dual questions about profit—how much to aim for and how to distribute it—is well overdue.

REFERENCES

1. *BIM Bulletin* (1973) vol. 6, no. 2, pp. 2 - 3.
2. Flew, A. (1973) *The Profit Motive. Foundation for Business Responsibilities,* London.

CHAPTER 7

Serving Peoples and Nations Everywhere

TOO MUCH POWER?

The title of this chapter happens to be the motto of ITT (the International Telephone and Telegraphic Corporation), but it may well be claimed by many other giant companies as their creed, particularly those whose interests straddle many countries. Not unnaturally, the strength and power of these large companies have generated a great deal of suspicion and criticism from many circles: from politicians, who are worried about the effect of international transactions on the economies of individual states; from industralists, who fear the erosion of fair competition inherent in the potential power of overt or concealed monopolies; from trade union leaders, who are incensed by the ability of large corporations to switch production or investment from one country to another, a feature that unions suspect is designed to weaken their bargaining position; and from students of social affairs, who are concerned about the social implications of centralization of power and decision-making, which many perceive as an alarming and often an inevitable consequence of corporation size.

Size is indeed one of the main causes for concern. It has been pointed out often enough that some of the large corporations have turnovers that exceed those of national budgets: the General Motors Corporation has an annual income greater than the GNP of Belgium, Denmark, Holland, Switzerland, or Sweden; even ITT, which is only a quarter the size of General Motors (in terms of sales income), has a revenue that exceeds the GNP of Greece, Norway (before the oil boom), or Portugal. That these giant corporations can have a significant effect on the economies of some of the countries in which they operate is quite evident, and questions must therefore arise as to how they can and do use the economic power that they inevitably must hold.

Of course, in considering international operations there are many variations on the theme: there are international companies, multi-national companies, and trans-national companies. The variations reflect different approaches to internal structure, to control methods of operations (and hence to the degree of centralization), and to the allegiance to the countries in which they operate (as opposed to the country in which they are registered and have their headquarters). Even the problems of definition have not yet been fully mastered, and arguments still rage as to what precisely an international company is and how it can be differentiated from any other. Definitions are clearly of some consequence if any legislation is attempted to constrain and/or encourage the operations of such companies.

Another cause for concern is the range of their activities. Some—like the oil companies—are narrowly based (relatively) in terms of the range of products and services with which they are involved. Others are conglomerates with wide ranging interests. ITT, for example, covers a curious variety of activities: from telephones to insurance, from hotels to fire extinguishers, from car hire to cosmetics. Where precisely is the synergy that is claimed for the merger operations avidly pursued by conglomerates? Does it simply lie in the financing ability of an essentially holding company, which can also provide professional expertise to its subsidiaries (such as legal services, know-how on taxation problems, market intelligence information, management services), or is it that the conglomerate can offer a captive market to its own subsidiaries (all members of the group "encouraged" to use only the services of its own hotel chain, its own insurance company, its own car-hire facility)? The former is legitimate, if evidence can be put forward to substantiate the argument; the latter is ominous, at least to those who abhor monopolies and wish to resist any restrictive segmentation of the market that militates against freedom of choice.

BUSINESS AND POLITICS

But above all it is the question of relationships with governments and political parties that has been scrutinized at some length. Can and does a giant corporation affect political issues, even elections? Can it extract concessions and special treatment from a government by striking a sinister deal that distorts the democratic and judicial process? Can it so manipulate the environment in which it operates to the extent that instead of it "serving people and nations everywhere" it becomes served by people and nations everywhere?

It is perhaps this aspect of ITT's behaviour that Anthony Sampson is most concerned about in his recent book *The Sovereign State* (Hodder & Stoughton, 1973). The sub-title of the book, *The Secret History of ITT*, turns out to be an exaggeration, since the book does not produce any startling revelations about ITT's political activities that are not available from proceedings of testimonies and documents presented before various senate committees in the United States, and other historical details about the expansion of ITT and the record of its acquisitions can hardly be described as secret.

Not surprisingly, the author concentrates on events and disclosures that led to two serious allegations about ITT; the first concerns its offer to make a handsome donation to the Republican Convention in 1972, which strangely coincided with the settlement of an outstanding anti-trust action against the Corporation; and the second that it was involved—in collaboration with the CIA—in activities intended to prevent Allende from being elected President of Chile in 1970. But Sampson refers to some wider issues associated with large corporations; for example, in discussing the disagreements among economists during the sixties as to what should be done about conglomerates, he says:

"The case against conglomerates was not indeed an easy one to make, for by their diversity they cut across the old definitions of monopoly and restriction of trade; and it was partly to avoid anti-trust action that they had become so diversified. Few of them dominated a single industry, and theoretically world industry might be run by a handful of vast conglomerates, each competing with scores of industries, without cutting across anti-trust laws. The fundamental argument against them was not so much economic, as political and social: that they restricted individuality and freedom of choice, that they centralised and concentrated activities which could survive separately, that they were simply, in a word, too big, too ubiquitous and too powerful. But that was a charge that was hard to define in legal terms."

In the 1962 annual report to the shareholders of ITT, it was stated that over the years the Corporation has

"met and surmounted every device employed by governments to encourage their own industries and hamper those of foreigners, including taxes, tariffs, quotas, currency restrictions, subsidiaries, barter arrangements, guarantees, moratoriums, devaluation—yes, and nationalization."

Nothing could so succinctly describe the blatant and inherent conflict of interests between the giant international corporation and countries in which it operates. It is this conflict of interests, which can be sharpened by changes in regimes and attitudes to foreign investments or to monopolies, that is the natural cause for corporations taking defensive action to protect their investments and future prosperity. And indeed one cannot blame them. The number of examples in recent years of countries expropriating investments of foreign companies with derisory or no compensation is bound to alarm most chief executives with overseas investments and this explains—even if it does not always justify—the actions taken by the companies in question.

The characteristic of ITT that struck Sampson most when he started his study of that "arcane organogram", as he put it, was its being a "self contained world" (hence the title of the book *The Sovereign State*), an impregnable castle with its own ethics and rituals, its own goals and control systems, its own unmistakable identity. And this is reflected in the relationships between representatives of the Corporation and other bodies abroad, as pointed out by Mueller (the former chief economist of the Federal Trade Commission in the United States, quoted in the 1971 Conglomerate Report) regarding local dignitaries and public figures on ITT boards: "It is not unfair to ask, are such men on ITT's board because of their business acumen or their prestige in international diplomacy?" Is their loyalty primarily to their own country or to ITT? What interests do they precisely represent at home and abroad? These are questions which become increasingly difficult to answer when the corporation gets overtly embroiled in political and socio-economic problems. Sampson ends on the right note when he says:

"The behaviour of ITT as it emerged by accident to the public is not, I hope, typical of multinationals: but it is an example of how deeply communications can be corrupted, like a poisoned well: and how easily, without countervailing power, the strength of multinationals can be abused. The worries it induces can only be allayed by the corporations (including of course ITT) taking the initiative, in exposing themselves more honestly before the public, before they are compelled to."

CONTROL AND RISK OF FAILURE

One of the intriguing facets of the ITT story is recounted by Sampson in a chapter entitled "The moving finger", in which he describes the monthly review meetings in Brussels, involving 120 people scrutinizing a continuous stream of statistical tables flashed on a screen. An arrow ("the moving finger") moves relentlessly from line to line, pausing for an explanation whenever performance appears to deviate from an expected standard, followed by a further cross-examination of the executive responsible for the activity in question. A better example of the satisficing philosophy in action would be difficult to elicit, with management control being almost entirely based on the exception principle, giving the best possible incentive for managers to conform, and indeed wherever possible to advocate "reasonable" targets, which would not be too difficult to attain. It is an illusion to suggest that better control in such an environment can only be achieved by an elaborate paperwork system, although this is what often happens with the centralization of decision-making and strategy planning. What are the implications of such procedures for the long term well-being of the company, for its stability and for inter-personal relationships within it? This is surely a fascinating area for investigation and research.

Sampson's book is, of course, not the first to draw attention to the political activities of corporations and their implications to our society; it is a subject of great fascination (not only to journalists), when secret and sensational information comes to light. But there is another problem that has perhaps not been sufficiently ventilated, and that concerns the possible social and economic dangers to society when a large and complex system, like one of the giant corporations, simply ceases to function, not necessarily because of evil or sinister intentions of their leaders, not because their goals could be in conflict with national interests, but because of technical malfunctioning of the system. Now, it may be argued that such a catastrophe is just not likely to happen, that large corporations like IBM or

Unilever or ITT are too robust to be vulnerable to outside disturbances or to internal failures in their control systems. Yet, large-scale and complex systems do fail, and they do go astray. The failure of the electric supply system on the eastern seaboard in the United States in 1967 was totally unexpected, so were the sudden collapse of the Penn Central in 1970 and the upheavals at IOS. The possible consequences of such a failure, and the ripple effect on the rest of the economy, with governments having to nationalize the enterprise in question, should perhaps be considered in greater depth than hitherto. We do not always know when economies of scale cease and the risks of size begin.

CHAPTER 8

How Society Works

"In any society, individuals and social groups are bound to conflict over goals, priorities and their share of available resources. But they can still live tolerably well together if they accept certain minimal rules and principles which inescapably govern how their society functions." This is how Sir Charles Goodeve introduces a booklet entitled *How Society Works*, recently published by OPUS, an Organization for Promoting the Understanding of Society (1975, London). The purpose of the booklet is to enunciate some general principles that apply to society—any society—so that its workings will thereby become better understood (the booklet is even sub-titled *The need for wider understanding*). Eleven principles are proposed:

"1. Goods and services cannot be used or consumed unless they have been produced and made available.

"2. Except in times of surplus, an increase in any one person's or group's consumption, if not matched by increased production, reduces the goods and services available for consumption by all other people in the same distribution area by the same total amount.

"3. Of the total effort and resources available, a higher proportion can be devoted to consumption.

"4. Prices cannot be held below costs.

"5. Man has the capacity to take in information, assess this in relation to his previous learning and choose a line of action in the light of his recognition of the related restraints and pressures. His choice usually indicates what he thinks will bring an outcome most advantageous to himself.

"6. Membership of a group is both a means through which the individual achieves his objectives and also a constraint on his choices, in that he experiences pressures towards conformity to group standards and towards co-operation with his fellows.

"7. Individuals, groups and organizations tend to cope with conflict by denying responsibility for their actions and passing on the responsibility to others.

"8. All known systems of distribution of goods and services and of jobs are composed of two basic systems: (a) the market choice system; (b) the allocation system.

"9. For any one country, total outward payments (such as for imports, capital investment and lending abroad) always balance inward payments (for exports and for borrowing and gifts).

"10. Man feels a strong need to control those events which have most effect upon his own well-being and societies usually give him some degree of such power through ownership.

"11. The more an individual has of material things or power the easier it is for him to gain the next increment of having."

THREE TYPES OF PRINCIPLES

These principles are regarded by the authors as fundamental to the study of conflict and as independent of value judgement. They are proposed as laws based on logic and experience, being laws of nature, or simple statements of arithmetic, or man-made laws, although it is not always clear which of the principles fall into each of the three categories. Methodologically such identification may be of some importance since a law is, in fact, a model: it implies relationships between several entities which are mutually exclusive in their definition, so that knowledge of given changes in some will lead us to certain expectations regarding the others. If such a law is a law of nature, then man can predict the expected values of particular variables and the outcome of any actions that he may take within the system governed by that law; he may even be able to determine ways in which he can bring about a desired outcome.

A man-made law, however, implies acquiescence by all members of society, or at least by all members of a given system, to play by the rules, man-made rules, designed to determine causal relationships and outcomes. Here man can affect the system in two ways: first by his actions (as in the case of laws of nature), and secondly by a changing attitude to the rules (involving attempts to reinterpret, modify, or even abrogate them altogether). Thus, prediction of outcomes where man-made laws are concerned, involves an additional element of uncertainty regarding the "rules of the game" and the extent to which they are likely to continue to hold in any given situation. Indeed, the rules themselves may become a function of circumstances and subject to random effects, this may partly be the reason for man's behaviour being sometimes regarded as totally unpredictable.

A law which is neither a law of nature nor man-made is often easily recognizable as a tautological statement. It is not a law in the sense that it reveals any new relationships between variables, it merely restates definitions proposed for these variables; its main purpose is reinforcement, a useful device in human communications, but the term "law" would be a misnomer, at best we could call it a "tautological law".

This distinction between natural laws, man-made laws, and tautological laws underlines the suggestion that the first category is of a more lasting nature, the second is subject to change even in the short term, and the third is a matter of semantics. To enunciate laws which are entirely free of judgement and independent of culture, religious creed or political persuasion, one would have to confine one's efforts to natural laws, and the authors of the OPUS document cannot be said to have done only that.

VALIDITY AND SCOPE

And the resultant mixture has a symptomatic undulating level of rigour. Principle 2, for example, that when a static cake (total consumption) is divided among several groups, a greater share for one means a smaller share for another, is no more than a corollary of Principle 1 (worth restating nonetheless). Principle 5 either implies that man can ascertain his objectives in advance, and that he can (and does) systematically scrutinize alternative courses of action open to him and then behaves rationally in making a choice that will be most advantageous in terms of these objectives—a rather debatable premise—or that whatever outcome he manages to achieve is then defined as his stated objective—in which case we have an example of a tautological law.

Similarly, Principle 10 is somewhat obscure in that it does not properly define ownership: if what is meant is ownership of assets (such as the means of production), then hard evidence is distinctly lacking in support of the contention made; if the term also covers ownership of one's labour, then this is something that individuals have always had, and the increasing power of organized labour stems not from change of ownership but from the ability to control union membership; but possibly there is some confusion here between power and responsibility, and perhaps the intention of this Principle is first to convey the message that those who exercise power to influence events should develop a sense of responsibility and should be made accountable for the outcome of their actions, since the irresponsible use of power is a recipe for tyranny and exploitation, and secondly to suggest that ownership of assets (as, for example, in co-operatives) and/or profits enhances responsibility. As for Principle 11 the authors go on to say that society now impedes the divergent flow of individuals to the opposite extremes of wealth and poverty through graded tax systems, death duty, and provision of welfare, but they should have added the well-worn phrase "all things being equal". This Principle does not explain why the accepted tendency for the rich to become richer and for the poor to become poorer has not resulted in the total extinction of the middle class prior to, say, 1940 (since the impeding actions of society to which the authors allude have become paramount only during the last four decades or so), and this suggests that all things had indeed not been equal.

But it is not my intention to undertake a meticulous examination of each of the eleven principles and to dissect each at length as to its validity or the rigour of its presentation. The mixture of disciplines of the unnamed authors may explain the differences in formulation of the principles in terms of style and emphasis, and rather than dwell on the chosen eleven one might wonder about many that could be added to this list, such as:

- man's behaviour is often dictated by his role and not only by his personality
- evaluation of performance can only be done against predetermined targets and yardsticks (or: unless you know where you are going, how will you know when you have arrived?)

- power corrupts; checks and balances are needed to control it
- processes in socio-economic systems are often irreversible, and when they are reversible there is a hysteresis effect (or: things are not what they used to be)
- there is always a conflict between the short term and the long term (this is perhaps a more general statement than Principle 3)
- most industrial situations are not zero-sum games, and strategies of envy or maximization of self-interest are not always best in terms of outcomes

RATIONAL MAN

One could go on, and the authors of the OPUS document would undoubtedly be delighted to examine new propositions and add to their magnificent eleven. But it seems that a much more fundamental question needs to be asked: What is the precise purpose of these principles? If it is to enlarge our knowledge and understanding of society, then this is laudable enough. But the OPUS pamphlet is much more explicit in its objective, and apart from urging all responsible people in society to communicate these proposed principles to the populace at large, it ends up with the statement: "A better understanding will reduce conflict and release additional resources of energy to contribute to a more constructive and happier society."

This is a typical positivist - rationalist view, commonly held by students of the industrial scene; it is the school of thought that believes that problems facing society can be formulated and analysed in a systematic way, that when a number of courses of action is available it is desirable to examine them in terms of their relative merits and outcomes and that it is therefore possible to identify the best alternatives as judged by predefined criteria, that once an optimal solution to a given problem is determined it should be embraced and implemented—in short this school of thought believes in rational man.

What we need to ask ourselves is, first, whether rational man is a realistic proposition, and secondly whether—assuming rational man is adopted as a working hypothesis—the result would be an elimination or at least a reduction of conflict. As for the first, it involves not only the assumption that rationality is universal and impersonal, that it is capable of a dispassionate determination in each case, that it is culture-free, and that what is seen as rational by one individual will be readily (or after discussion) accepted as rational by another, but also that once an individual recognizes what is a rational thing to do he will indeed do it. We know, alas, that neither accords with everyday experience. Arguments do persist about what solution logic should dictate, and no analysis of socio-economic and managerial problems is entirely value-free. Whether this state of affairs stems entirely from lack of agreement on goals (where it is not difficult to see that value judgement is bound to play an important part), or whether the choice of analytical tools also contributes to a potential discord, is a matter for debate; but the fact remains that we often encounter disparities in views, both concerning how problems should be defined and how they should be solved. And with regard to human behaviour, deviations from what appears to be rational choice are observed often enough, either because of inadequacy or ambiguity in goal definition, or for reasons of personality and other forces which may even be unconnected with the goals in question.

The second question alluded to earlier is whether rational behaviour is bound to reduce conflict. If we adopt a rationalistic viewpoint we have to accept that when a problem has a single optimal solution and if the interested parties come to realize and accept its logic, any conflict between them will automatically be dissipated. But it is similarly inevitable that when there is no single solution, that when one party can·inflict incalculable damage on another in the pursuit of its own interests, it will indeed proceed to do so, and under those circumstances (which often occur in non-zero-sum games) rationality in the sense understood here will only exacerbate conflict rather than abate it.

CONFLICT THEORIES

It is indeed curious how diverse are the prevailing views on the question of conflict and its resolution, as suggested by the following spectrum:

(1) the one happy family theory
(2) the paternalistic theory
(3) the consensus theory
(4) the conflict resolution theory
(5) the continuing conflict theory

The first is held by those who are perturbed by the whole notion of conflict and who seek to avoid it either by denying that it exists or by trying to dismiss its implications. They argue that there is much more that unites employers and employees than divides them, that in the face of the overwhelming importance of their common goals sectional interests shrink into insignificance, and that the "working together" ethic is an essential element in the maxim that prevention is better than cure. And as long as prevention works, this theory is commendable enough, but it is impotent when conflict does arise because it does not explicitly address itself to the problem of distribution of profit and power in the industrial enterprise.

The paternalistic theory takes the view that an industrial conflict generally involves two very unequal contestants, so unequal that one can be completely crushed by the other. The dominant contestant must, therefore, be aware of his power and show compassion by voluntarily allowing the weaker side to obtain greater benefits than those that he would have to be content with if judged solely by the power balance in the struggle. In years gone by it was the employers who had to exercise such a paternalistic role (albeit not always wisely); in modern times the power balance has shifted quite considerably, but those who hold to the paternalistic theory would argue that its message remains valid irrespective of which side is dominant in a particular struggle.

The consensus theory looks for a resolution of conflict in a way that is generally thought to be fair. It maintains that justice need not only be done but must also be seen to be done; that it is neither acceptable for the strong to impose their will on the weak nor is it sufficient for the strong to be magnanimous in a paternalistic fashion. Furthermore, a consensus of what is fair is not a matter to be confined to the parties involved in the conflict; since it is rare in modern industrial society for one sector to be totally immune from the repercussions of what happens in another, it is essential for outsiders to the conflict (outsiders with varying degrees of objectivity) to accept that justice has been done. It is not, of course, easy to determine in each case what the consensus is—the press and broadcasting media are both a help and a hindrance in this respect—but, as believers in the consensus theory will argue, this is a technical problem, which does not in itself invalidate the need for consensus; without it, resentment and enmity may ensue, sowing the seeds for fresh and even more bitter struggles in the future.

A consensus solution, however, is not necessarily a rational solution; since a consensus inevitably involves taking the temperature of a political climate, particularly when major issues are involved, the recommended solution may well be influenced by strong emotions and transient considerations.

Rational man will argue that no solution can have a lasting value unless the problem has been looked at dispassionately, that if reason is not satisfied, objections to the solution are bound to persist. It is far more profitable, therefore, to resort to logic and solve a given problem once and for all, in the same way that we solve mathematical problems under given premises. This conflict resolution theory has its attractions, but it suffers from two shortcomings: first, industrial problems (unlike mathematical problems) rarely have generally recognized premises and agreement needs to be reached about these premises before an analytical examination can be undertaken (and, alas, people's preferred premises may be affected by their expectations of the resultant solutions), and secondly for many non-zero-sum games there are no agreed analytical solutions, and questions of judgement and personal preferences regarding methods of co-operation between the players may thus remain.

Finally, the continuing conflict theory is not suggested as a substitute for the other theories but as a supplement. It simply points out that a conflict is never finally resolved, that as soon as a solution is adopted for a given situation, new problems arise, and either the conflict re-emerges under a new guise or new conflicts are generated. It is therefore idle to pretend that any given conflict is an isolated static affair; it is but an element in an evolutionary process and hence it follows that whatever method is used to resolve a particular conflict, any bargaining that is employed, any consensus that is sought, should take account of the dynamic nature of conflict development and the changing forces that shape it.

Having said all this I must again concede that, while I continue to have reservations about the particular set of the OPUS principles, a case can obviously be made for attempts to improve our knowledge and understanding in this area. There is no guarantee that such knowledge will always be used to the good; indeed, it would be surprising if it were not deliberately misused by the greedy and the unscrupulous, in the same way that all knowledge has been misused in one way or another during the history of mankind. There is no guarantee, therefore, that society will be any the better for knowing how it works, and there is certainly no guarantee that industrial conflict can thereby be reduced. And thus, in the application of whatever knowledge we manage to gain, it is well to beware the pitfalls inherent in any of the theories of conflict resolution and to counsel caution. Attitudes of rationality, tolerance, moderation, and compassion are not always compatible, yet they all need to be exercised in the management of industrial affairs; alas, not one of the theories can claim to encourage all these attitudes to such a degree that it could be totally embraced on its own.

CHAPTER 9

On Education in Management Science

The process of establishing management studies as a recognized academic discipline has been fraught with numerous difficulties. Even in the United States with its very long tradition of tolerating these studies in the academic environment, where expansion of university activity in this area has been quite phenomenal since World War II, the arguments as to the scope and content of management studies have not abated, and will probably continue to rage for many years to come. The plethora of programmes, even the variety of titles used to describe them, is evidence of the divergence of views held on this subject. There are programmes of business administration run by powerful and popular business schools, there are programmes in operational research, in management science, in industrial management, in industrial engineering—to mention just some of the prevalent titles. They all have their own philosophies, their own emphases on what is regarded as a relevant range of subjects that students should cover in some depth if they aspire to practise in some aspect of management during their future careers. In presenting my own personal views on this subject I do not wish to suggest that I regard other approaches as spurious or invalid; indeed, it would be a sad day when all of us have precisely the same viewpoint and run the same programmes. We must agree to disagree, and it is only in this way that experimentation and re-examination of our values and objectives can take place.

A useful starting point in discussing management education is to ask questions about the management task. Management science, operational research, business administration—call it what you like—is concerned with the analysis of alternative courses of action, of planning, and of execution. It is the art of the possible and the attainable. It should not be concerned just with what managers actually do in the course of their work, but in the main with what managers can and should do. The ability to pose penetrating questions and to solve them, the ability to create new opportunities, the ability to project and to implement—these are the attributes that we identify with the task of management.

To perform this task in a manner that would win the acclaim of dispassionate critics, the manager needs to have certain qualities and be equipped with various tools, and these may perhaps be conveniently grouped as follows:

(1) Capacity for analysis.
(2) Knowledge of operational methods.
(3) Experience.
(4) Personal characteristics.

First, the manager must have a capacity for analysis. He needs to know how to set and interpret objectives and information, how to examine their compatibility, how to define problems, how to construct a model of a system as a means of studying its behaviour, how to infer from the particular about the general, how to specify alternative courses of action.

Secondly, he needs to have a substantive knowledge of operational methods—physical and managerial—that can be employed by the organization in pursuit of its objectives. The physical methods include, for example, the production processes by which a product can be manufactured, bearing in mind its purpose and design characteristics. The managerial processes involve the design and use of procedures by which the activities of the company can be controlled, and understanding of the workings of administrative functions such as finance, personnel, marketing, production, etc., and the means by which all these functions are integrated in the organization structure. An intimate knowledge of operational methods is, therefore, indispensable to the manager, and by this we mean not only an insight into what such methods can do, but—equally important—what they cannot do. The recognition and specification of constraints in the system under the manager's control, particularly constraints pertaining to the use of resources, is an important component of the task of management.

And, thirdly, he needs to have experience. The ability to draw conclusions from one situation to another, the ability to identify symptoms in any given situation—these skills are effectively acquired and enhanced by experience, provided of course that the manager has not lost the capacity to learn from his successes and failures.

Fourthly, he needs to have certain personal qualities: he must be able to communicate his ideas to others, to get on with his fellow-men, to have the social skills that are needed in maintaining appropriate human relationships, to possess that quality which is so elusive to define—leadership; he must be decisive and willing to take risks, and he must be prepared to take full responsibility for his actions.

These are the skills and attributes of the manager. How can an educational programme be designed to meet these needs?

In the first place we should recognize that not all these attributes can and need to be developed as a result of an educational programme. Attributes of experience and personality are particularly difficult to impart during a course of study: experienced men can talk about their experience to students; a variety of problems and situations can be simulated through case studies, business games, and other exercises; social skills in communication can certainly be developed and improved; but there are real limitations to the extent to which progress in these matters can be made. And even if it were possible to achieve far-reaching results, e.g. in changing the personality of students in a significant way, I would regard such casting of students in some predetermined mould as morally indefensible.

Even with regard to such attributes as the capacity for analysis and the need for knowledge of operational methods, we must recognize the limitations of any educational programme. To enhance the student's ability to analyse and solve problems there are certain specific actions that can be taken: he can be taught methods of analysis, techniques of operational research, mathematics, the structure of models, and the procedures useful to employ in building them. He can be taught how to recognize significant facets of problems, how to categorize them, and how to use systematic (and often programmable) methods for solving them. We have reason to believe that such knowledge and understanding will stand the student in good stead when he faces new problems, which require a fresh approach or a novel method of solution. It is conceivable, of course, that the student's analytical faculties can be sharpened more effectively by other means, e.g. by solving riddles, studying Latin, spending time on jigsaw puzzles, or playing chess. But such an argument is not confined to the management area and would be equally valid in any field of human endeavour. It would seem, therefore, that in concentrating on analytical tools that are found to be relevant and applicable in solving managerial problems, we are providing effective and sufficient opportunities for an analytical capability to be developed.

There is also a limit on the knowledge of operational methods that can be imparted in an academic programme, simply because of its limited duration. While no one can deny that knowledge of the scope of production processes and their limitations is useful information for the manager, it would be impractical to run lengthy courses on every known process in every single industry in order to ensure that the graduate is well prepared for any conceivable eventuality. Similarly, it is impossible within the time constraints to turn out a graduate who is specialized in every single function of business. Some selection of the enormous amount of material associated with these functions and with administrative procedures is inevitable. The question is: How is this selection to be done?

One is driven to the conclusion that the purpose of an academic programme in management is not to turn out full-blooded qualified managers. Indeed, it cannot be. Apart from time limitations, which are serious enough, there are fundamental doubts as to whether such a programme is able to impart to its participants all the desirable attributes. It is naïve to regard such a programme as a mere conversion facility which produces raring-to-go finished managers, ready to be slotted into an organization and to take on managerial duties; raring-to-go they may be, but whether they are finished and ready is another matter.

In constructing a programme in management we can only hope that the student emerges much better prepared to embark on a career in this field, and the subject matter for such a programme must represent some balance between the following four categories:

(1) Supporting subjects, the basic knowledge of which is required in order to study at a reasonable level some subjects in other categories. Mathematics, probability and statistics, computing, sociology and psychology may all be regarded as supporting subjects.
(2) Subjects relating to the external environment, in which the industrial firm has to operate, such as general economic theory, fiscal policy, taxation, industrial and international law, politics, and others.
(3) Subjects relating to the internal environment of the firm, such as operational research, managerial economics, organization theory, and each of the functional areas of the firm.

(4) Subjects which may be included in the programme in order to
    "liberalize" the student, such as philosophy, the arts, and languages.

Opinions as to the right balance between these various subjects will vary.
Category 3 is clearly the *raison d'être* of a programme in the management
field, but if it is constructed to the exclusion of others, it is bound to
become rather self-centred and somewhat dull. It is impossible, however,
to be dogmatic about the amount of time that a student should ideally
spend on subjects in each category, except perhaps to suggest that the
treatment of few subjects with rigour and in depth is preferable and has a
more lasting effect than coverage of numerous topics rather superficially.
For the same reason I also believe in devoting a substantial amount of time
to quantitative methods.

There are two extreme approaches that can be adopted in the design of
the curriculum, the one may be termed the single programme approach,
and the other is the modular approach. The first presents a carefully
thought-out range of subjects which—however arbitrary their choice may
seem—every student must take. "They may not see the relevance now, but
given time they will begin to appreciate the benefit of discipline and
rigour." The second approach is to present a wide range of subjects from
which students have to make a selection, and the choice may be so wide
that two students emerging from the same programme may have covered
mutually exclusive sets of subjects. The disadvantage of the first approach
lies in its rigidity and inability to accommodate varying interests; the
shortcomings of the second lie in the programme being so fragmented as to
lose any sense of structural unity. Many universities, therefore, have
come to realize the advantages of a compromise: a core of compulsory
subjects that ensures a minimum substantive knowledge in key areas,
coupled with a range of elective subjects to cater for diverse interests and
for the need for specialization.

I am also in favour of a student project in the Master's programme.
Even with a massive shift from formal teaching to seminars, case studies,
and assignments, all of which help to achieve a high degree of student participation, a problem-oriented project provides the student with valuable
experience. He has to go through the agonies of continuously reappraising
and reformulating his problem, and he faces an intellectual challenge that
forces him to delve into one area in some depth. The critics will argue
that the student project is often very narrowly defined, that the time spent

on the project could perhaps be better employed in broadening the student's knowledge in skills in other fields, that the supervision effort is prohibitively expensive. I recognize the substance of these weighty arguments, but on balance I believe that—for the reasons mentioned earlier—the student project is a useful component for which time should be allocated in the programme.

Throughout this discussion there appears to be no distinction between the management scientist and the aspiring manager. This is not because I fail to recognize the difference between the two roles: the management scientist is the man who analyses a problem in some depth and recommends a course of action, while the manager is the one who takes the decision. The measure of responsibility for one's actions is clearly very different for the two, so to some extent are the personal qualities needed for the job. And yet it does not follow that this difference necessarily implies that we should construct two distinctly different Master's programmes to suit two brands of people. First, it is difficult to identify at the beginning of a course those students who are destined for line management as opposed to functional management or management science, and secondly it may be argued that a spell as management scientists is probably an excellent apprenticeship for those who aspire to line management.

So much for the Master's programme, but what about the Doctoral programme? I confess that I am not convinced by the generally held view that the sole purpose of a Doctoral programme in management science is to produce teachers of management. Admittedly, the holder of a Doctoral degree has presumably demonstrated a high level of ability in a given field of study and his proven intellectual capacity is a valuable asset for the management teacher; but to make the PhD degree the only licence to teach—as appears to be the tendency at present—is to take an unjustifiably extreme position. One can think of attributes other than excellence in research in a narrow field which make for a good teacher, and similarly there is no reason to suggest that the PhD should not be an equally valuable asset for certain positions in industry.

There are real dangers in many schools where the Doctoral programmes have become self-perpetuating mechanisms, constantly feeding on themselves. Their research and teaching become entirely divorced from the industrial environment and centre on an emasculated pseudo-world of their own creation. If management science is to be concerned with management, then all the arguments pertaining to the management task are equally relevant to the Doctoral programme. The central characteristics of the Doctoral programme revolve around the need to specialize and to demonstrate competence and independent thought in research. Such attributes imply that the student is capable (with help and supervision) of charting his own way and fending for himself, and this suggests that the research element should be predominant in the programme compared with the formal course component. An examination of many Doctoral programmes reveals that about one-third of the time is spent on research, while some two-thirds are spent on formal course work. I wonder whether it would not be appropriate for this balance to be reversed.

There is at present a wide and legitimate gap between the MSc and the PhD and this gap can usefully be filled by an interim degree; in the University of London such a degree (the MPhil) was introduced a few years ago. Like the PhD the MPhil is a research degree, but it requires only two years (compared with three to four for the PhD) and it provides an excellent framework for those people who are unable or unwilling to subject themselves to the more strenuous requirements of a PhD programme. Many holders of MPhil degrees would want to take up management education as a career, while others may aspire to have senior positions in management science in industry.

As for the research task of the PhD/MPhil candidate, it should not necessarily demonstrate his capacity for hard work, as his contribution to knowledge in the field of his research, and his ability to do original work. I am not so much concerned as to whether this research is primarily technique-oriented or problem-oriented. There is room and a need for both types of research in management science.

CHAPTER 10

Management Careers for Management Scientists

Many industrial enterprises run a "management training" scheme. Its purpose is to process newly recruited graduates through a programme, usually of one to two years' duration, to expose them to the management milieu and to explain to them what the management task is all about. More often than not the new recruits have no prior knowledge or understanding of the business world, their university degree may be quite remote from the main activities of the firms they join; indeed, some firms positively prefer to recruit arts graduates, in the belief that moulding fresh young starry-eyed innocents to suit their needs is more profitable than taking on hard-nosed engineers and scientists with an allegedly narrow outlook, and possibly more advantageous than business or management science graduates, who think they know all the answers and have inflated expectations. In any event, the intake of these new graduates is bound to be non-homogeneous, representing varied background and interests, so that the device of a management training scheme appears to be an effective unifying induction process.

The scheme is often modelled on the well-tried apprenticeship formula (for many years the standard training process of professional engineers in Britain), which usually consists of four components: the first is concerned with basic courses in certain skills and techniques (typical examples include principles of accounting, planning and control, organizational behaviour, use of computers, report writing, and communications); the second consists of an introduction to the firm, its organization and ethos, often involving subtle (and, sometimes, not subtle) indoctrination; the third is a "milk-round" involving a tour of some key departments and production or service centres, each trainee spending several weeks at each point to see how departments operate and also to get to know people at the middle-management hierarchy; and the fourth component may consist of a project, carried out individually, or as part of a team, culminating in a written and sometimes also a verbal report.

Having completed this programme, the trainee is then asked to signify which department or function he would like to join and, assuming that a suitable vacancy exists and that he is acceptable to the manager of that department or function, the first appointment of the trainee on the managerial ladder takes place.

This somewhat brief description of the management training scheme does not do justice to the many variations on the theme that are found in industry, to the different emphases given by particular companies to the general versus the specialist nature of the training (or vice versa), to the intricacies in design of the "milk-round", to the type and purpose of the project carried out by the trainee, to the degree the programme is tailored to suit the individual. But all these variations have a common basic philosophy—that of recruiting people to man the management line and staff structure, not immediately but after a decent spell of induction and mutual observation.

This training process "on the job" focuses on management as it is, on the reality and environment within which the firm operates, on the array of problems with which its managers have to cope. When the management trainee becomes a junior manager, he is gently "tuned in" to the current problems associated with his first appointment and to the prevailing procedures for handling them. The training scheme also provides a convenient framework for career planning: the uniform intake simplifies the design of the salary structure offered to trainees, and with a firm foothold on the bottom rung of the managerial ladder, they can look forward to steady progress for a number of years, the rate of advance and the ultimate prospects being adjusted to suit the capabilities and promise shown by each individual. In this way the organization can ensure that the occupant of a middle or senior management post has experience of particular positions at lower levels in the hierarchy, and indeed in such organizations the ambitious individual not only acquiesces with the organizational specifications for desirable career paths, he often positively seeks to gain the experience that is thought to be indispensable so as not to adversely affect his eligibility for future promotions.

In contrast to the management trainee scheme, which is concerned with management as it is, we have management education at universities, partly concerned with fundamental concepts, partly with development of methodology, and partly with management as it should be. By its very nature, university education in management is seldom focused on one industry, let alone one particular enterprise, and rather than impart some narrow skills of the trade, the emphasis is on the understanding of the environment, on appreciating constraints and identifying opportunities, on allocation of resources to meet certain ends, on modelling and analysis. Programmes in universities obviously vary: some are undoubtedly concerned more with training specific skills than others, some aim at producing a product that will be of immediate use in industry, some specialize in particular functions and their attendant methodology (such as finance, personnel, production, systems analysis). But inasmuch as generalizations in this respect are possible, management education at universities is largely aimed at producing the industrial leaders of the future, while management training schemes in industry are concerned with problems of the present.

It is often suggested that within this output from business and management programmes we need to differentiate between graduates of business schools and those who come out of universities with a management science (or operational research) qualification (usually with a second degree in that field). The former are perhaps more generalists, often with a first degree in arts or social sciences, perhaps more flexible as to what function or line position they should take, often more vague about the contribution they expect to make when they go into industry; the latter are more quantitatively inclined, more technique-ridden, often obsessed with modelling and detail, and usually fairly confident that their problem-orientated approach will make a contribution within a relatively short period of time.

Whether these distinctions are valid is an open question. Some business schools have developed specialisms in quantitative methods to an extent that their graduates would qualify for the title of management scientists, and the lines of demarcation between them and the genuine article become increasingly unreal. But be that as it may, the fact remains that when they go into industry, graduates in MS (Management Science) and OR (Operational Research), who for the sake of convenience will be referred to as "management scientists", tend to join MS and OR groups, whereas business graduates generally do not. And while industry has learnt, with varying degrees of indecision, how to absorb business graduates (particularly in countries like the United States, where business schools have been in existence for many decades), it is less certain that they are sufficiently prepared to cope with career problems for management scientists.

To begin with, we must realize that management scientists are not a uniform mass with respect to their interests and career aspirations. My contacts with such people (over a number of years) lead me to suggest that they fall into three categories: the first consists of those who are glad to have been exposed to modelling and analysis during their university course, but who do not wish to become OR analysts; they proceed to join industry in a line or staff function in the same way as other business graduates. The second category includes those who revel in model building and in the use of quantitative techniques; they are happy to remain OR analysts all their lives, deriving satisfaction from solving problems of increasing variety and complexity, and becoming OR managers charged with the supervision of others in their field.

Now, these two categories do not present serious problems in terms of career planning. The first joins the normal battle for recognition and promotion in the management structure, going as far as their capabilities and luck permit. The second category involves people akin to those employed in an R & D function, and the organization needs to devise a mechanism that allows their salaries to progress in keeping with their technical skills and contributions. But then there is a third category, larger perhaps than the other two, consisting of people who go into MS groups for several years, in some cases to become team or project leaders, even OR managers, and then want to move to general management. Many have such intentions from the moment they join the MS group, some develop a yen for managerial responsibility as they grow older. How should these aspirants be handled by the organization?

On the face of it, there should be no problem. The advantages of having the MS group as an appropriate means for management recruiting may be regarded as self-evident. Indeed, it is difficult to conceive of a more effective management training programme: the young recruit, with a good theoretical background, becomes a member of a group concerned with problem solving and is totally project-oriented; his work involves him in problem definition, in measurement, in analysis and evaluation; he is forced to understand the

framework within which the problem needs to be solved, to communicate
with managers, to realize the intricacies of data collection; he is exposed to
the baffling vagaries of human nature, to the political character of management forces in action, and to the need to be tactful and persuasive in making
recommendations and in implementation. What, may one ask, could be
better training for management than several increasingly demanding projects over, say, a two- to four-year period in the management science group?
It is certainly vastly superior to the management training scheme described
earlier, although it is not intended to replace it (as, for one thing, only a few
recruits with a first university degree are sufficiently mature or qualified to
join an MS group), and it ensures that the young analysts retain an objectivity and independence of mind that can be so easily eroded in the case of
management trainees or junior managers. By consciously using the MS group
as a management recruiting channel, the organization can attract able
young men and put them through a much more demanding test than a
trainee scheme can ever hope to achieve, and thus meet organizational needs
while fulfilling the aspirations of those analysts who are willing and capable
of pursuing a managerial career. Furthermore, the vitality of the MS group
is thereby maintained with new blood flowing into it as old hands get pro-
moted and absorbed into the organizational structure.

The attractions of such a scheme seem obvious enough, and yet in many
firms we encounter numerous problems in implementing it. The reasons for
the difficulties are multifarious, but three major barriers to the movement
of analysts out of an MS group should be singled out.

The first is the *salary barrier*. After a few years in an MS group, an
ambitious and energetic analyst is bound to make reasonable progress on
the salary scale, usually more so than a management trainee or a junior
manager, so that his salary and perhaps even managerial status tend to be
ahead of others of comparable age and experience. To move out of the MS
group and to retain his salary and status, let alone improve them, he expects
to be offered a position in the managerial hierarchy that is usually reserved
for a much older man. A "sideways" move or a "demotion" (even if it is
only in status without loss of pay) in order just to break away from the MS
group and its specialist label is often regarded as a traumatic experience,
both for the individual and for the organization.

And this leads us to the *tradition barrier*. In some firms no promotion
to certain positions or levels in the organization is possible for people who

have not followed certain rigidly prescribed career paths, involving spells of service in specified junior line and staff posts. Such constraints are based on sound historical reasons, with many precedents to support the argument that for senior managers to be effective they need to have had a good exposure to the "shop-floor" environment, where the actual work is done and where customers need to be satisfied.

The third is the *intellectual arrogance barrier*, which the management scientist often creates for himself. Having worked for a while in an intellectually stimulating environment in an MS group, having been in contact with senior managers in the course of his project work, it is natural for him to regard junior managerial posts as immersed in routine and relatively undemanding tasks; it is difficult for him to understand why he needs to spend several years of his life in such posts, just because they have become a prerequisite for future promotion, when he feels that his competence can be demonstrated in other ways. The organization does not take kindly to such sentiments, which it regards as sheer intellectual arrogance, and (if anything) its attitudes then tend to harden.

These barriers to mobility from the MS group to other parts of the organization are bound to lead to frustration for the young aspirant, and unless he is prepared to acquiesce in a vague hope of better things to come, he begins to look for opportunities elsewhere, and eventually the organization loses him altogether. But there is another and perhaps more serious consequence to such a state of affairs, namely that as ambitious young men get to know about potential obstacles to mobility, they may begin to wonder whether they should join the MS group in the first place. The effect on recruitment to the group could then be far reaching, both in terms of the quality and type of applicants. And, needless to say, if many firms experience such problems there could be dire consequences for management science in general.

How can these problems be resolved? I start with the premise that an MS group is indeed an effective training ground for future managers (i.e. for those management scientists who are willing and able to become managers) and that this would be reflected in the policy for recruitment to such a group. If this premise is endorsed by the organization, then several remedies spring to mind. First, it should be possible to arrange for secondment of the young management scientist for two or three spells of several weeks'/ months' duration outside the MS group, preferably in some line function.

(For example, he could act as an assistant to a line manager for a couple of months and then deputize for him when he goes on holiday or on a course.) Such exposure, albeit short, to the wider organizational environment, could be made a prerequisite to promotion even within the MS group; and it is bound to have a beneficial effect on the outlook of the group and may also help to abate criticisms of its remoteness. Thus, when the analyst completes his two- to four-year tour of duty as a management scientist and is ready to move on, he is less likely to be regarded as one totally lacking in relevant experience.

Secondly, an attempt must be made to encourage the management scientist to return to a senior appointment in the group a few years after leaving it. Such an arrangement will also help to destroy the myth of isolation, add maturity to the group, and enhance its acceptability to the more sceptical sections of the organization. A return to the MS group is, of course, not without its problems. After several years in a line position, the management scientist ceases to be a management scientist, he becomes more accustomed to the need to make decisions with very little information and often with inadequate amounts of analysis (inadequate from the scientist's viewpoint), he certainly finds it increasingly difficult to keep up with the literature. And so when an opportunity to return to the group as a manager materializes, there may be some reluctance on his part to take it up in preference to other possible openings. Provided the organization has a reasonable number of ex-management scientists of the right age and with the appropriate experience, and provided the appointment to the managerial echelons in the MS group is made sufficiently attractive, such possible difficulties can be overcome.

But in the main, the organization must make a deliberate attempt to remove the tradition barrier which was alluded to earlier. While specified career paths to reach the higher managerial echelons in the enterprise have a certain appeal, their logic is generally rooted in days gone by, their rigid interpretation may be less relevant for the present needs of most organizations, and a more flexible reappraisal of the policy they imply is often overdue. The rigidity with which these career paths are implemented in some large organizations is quite distressing. By the time a bright lad is supposed to have inched himself forward through a series of sometimes dreary junior and middle management posts to qualify for the top echelon, all the sap may have gone out of him, and he may have been transformed into an acceptable organization man, with no fire left in his belly. Now, some organizations thrive on such a process, but for most this is a dangerous recipe for inbred complacency. Sensible career-path-planning by all means, but let it be sufficiently flexible to overcome the problems of apathy and stagnation. Keynes once said (in a talk given in 1938) of himself and his friends as young men: "We entirely repudiated a personal liability on us to obey general rules. We claimed the right to judge every individual case on its merits and the wisdom, experience and self control to do so successfully." It is this spirit that the organization needs to maintain for its high-flyers, coupled with an opportunity to develop their insight and critical faculties, and where better to start than with its own management scientists?

CHAPTER 11

To Plead or not to Plead

Democracy demands that major decisions affecting the community and the environment should be subjected to scrutiny, not only after the decisions are made but also when they are contemplated. Armed with information on the reasons for giving decision-makers wanting to pursue certain courses of action, sections of the community can then react to the possible consequences of such actions, make suggestions of their own, and produce evidence in support of their arguments. By subjecting their proposals to open debate, the authorities provide an opportunity for contentious issues to be properly ventilated and attempt to ensure that the final decisions are seen to be for the common good and have the general approval of the public. In essence, this is the reason for the growing number of public inquiries, set up to investigate *ad hoc* issues, and permanent or semi-permanent bodies to monitor and adjudicate whenever major actions by government officials or business executives are likely to have a serious effect on the public interest.

Any dispassionate inquiry into such issues inevitably raises the problems of data and analysis. For example, if the subject of the inquiry is the siting of an airport, a power station, a production facility—questions immediately arise as to the need for such an installation, the cost to the community (financial cost, noise and inconvenience, effects on the environment), and the benefits to the community (creation of jobs, provision of products, or services by the new facility). For a cost - benefit analysis to be undertaken, the various factors—present and future—need to be quantified, so must be the corresponding factors relating to alternative solutions, as well as the consequences of taking no action at all. And these problems are exacerbated when the ex-

penditure of public money is contemplated and when some members of the
community feel that other causes have a stronger claim on available resources.

Two questions then arise: first, can management scientists help the
inquiry in the collection of relevant facts, and if so, how are they likely to
be regarded by the authorities conducting the inquiry? And secondly,
how should management scientists see their role in the analysis of data and
their interpretation, particularly when—as is ususally the case—various
opposing factions seek to protect their interests and to influence the inquiry
accordingly? In principle, one would think that management science has a
great deal to offer, although not enough cases have been documented in
sufficient detail to indicate what its intrinsic contribution (if any) has in
fact been.

One fascinating example in this respect is given in a recent account by
J. L. Steele.[1] It concerns the case of determining the price for natural gas
produced in the Permian Basin area in the United States and traces the
developments that led to the hearings before the Federal Power Commission
some years ago, when the Commission's Chief Economist introduced an
econometric model intended to relate supply, demand, and reserves of
natural gas to its price. Since the Commission, through its Examiner, needs
to weigh all the relevant evidence submitted at the hearings (which for
practical purposes may be regarded as similar to judicial proceedings), the
use of a quantitative model is clearly of some significant interest and has
implications for similar hearings before other agencies that determine rates
and prices, at least those associated with various utilities.

The exercise failed, and the Examiner ruled that "the econometric study
presented here is not relevant or material to the problem". Steele tries to
ascertain the reasons for the failure and the steps that should be taken in
such cases to foresee the pitfalls and sources of effective criticism. The
quantitative approach, exemplified in a model that attempts to establish
existing relationships and to forecast future consequences of given alternative policies, has an aura of objectivity about it, since it attempts to analyse
facts and to replace—at least in part—the subjective evidence of "experts"
If the model is properly constructed, it could be argued that its relevance
could not possibly be in doubt, indeed that the Examiner would have to
insist on it becoming an indispensable and integral part of the hearings.

[1] J. L. Steele (1974) OR models as tools for the regulation of industry, *Omega*,
vol. 2, pp. 335-47.

But such a procedure may—to some people—have the implication that the conclusions derived from the model become incontrovertible and may have to be regarded as equivalent to hard facts. Consequently, the Examiner may feel that he has less scope to exercise his judgement, and that matters that hitherto fell within his personal evaluation would become determined by mechanistic models or by precedents, where these models have been used and officially recognized. Add to that the fact that most Examiners are perhaps more versed with legal matters then with quantitative analysis (which often relies on unfamiliar mathematical manipulations), and it is not difficult to understand why an Examiner would be reluctant to abandon judgement for an impersonalistic - mechanical and often obscure tool.

This is a good example of a recurrent theme: as management science is applied in any area of human endeavour, it attempts to categorize, to quantify, to deduce relationships, to replace hunch with analysis, and as it proceeds along this path it encounters the natural resistance of those whose hunch and judgement and experience are apparently threatened. In practice, of course, the knowledge and capabilities of those concerned may be put to better use as a consequence, but they do not always perceive the possible effects in this way, nor is everyone adaptable enough to ensure that the transition will ultimately have beneficial effects for himself.

But this is only part of the story. As Steele points out, the analyst who constructs the model is both objective and subjective. He is objective in the sense that he attempts to state the problem and the relationships between variables in as precise and accurate a fashion as possible; he is subjective, however, in many of the assumptions that he makes, in the choice of analytical tools for the purpose, perhaps even in the choice of data considered relevant to a given model. One way to overcome these difficulties is to urge the analyst to build several models based on alternative sets of assumptions and use alternative methods of analysis, where more than one methodological approach is possible, to use all the data available, each set with accompanying qualifications as to its significance and accuracy, and thus produce several sets of results for the Examiner or the Judge to make a choice. But the very implication that there could be more than one answer to the problem under discussion may so undermine the whole quantitative approach as to strike at the heart of its intrinsic validity. And how is the Examiner to make his final choice? Unless he is sufficiently knowledgeable about the intricacies of various quantitative analyses, his expressed preference for one particular result and his rejection of another may well be spurious. If he asks the analyst to make the choice, he may feel that he is abdicating his own responsibility in this matter, and so the best that he can do is to have the analyst's recommendations and reasons as to which result should be accepted, and then judge for himself which arguments he finds convincing for a final choice to be made.

The assumption behind this approach is that the analyst is sufficiently knowledgeable, sufficiently scrupulous, and sufficiently motivated to produce all the alternative models and results. But what if he is not? Who will judge him and his competence? If one of the contestants in the case wishes to challenge him on professional and analytical grounds, should he be allowed to do so? In that case, what is the precise status of the "analyst of the commission" (or the court, for that matter)?

There is a very strong argument for allowing the contestants in such cases to have their own operational research analysts testify. This will bring the analysts into line with any other expert witnesses that give evidence before a court, in the same way it is possible for two experts in other fields to appear on behalf of rival interested parties, to look at the evidence from different angles, and to disagree with one another. Two lawyers appearing on behalf of their clients will each attempt to the best of his ability, but within given professional ethics, to present strong arguments and to persuade the court of the justice of his client's cause. So do professional expert witnesses, hired by both sides for the purpose, except that their role is to provide factual as well as subjective evidence, without being involved in the judicial pleading process. Why should OR (operational research) experts not be allowed to behave in a similar fashion?

Some would undoubtedly be horrified by such a prospect. The whole foundation of impartiality, objectivity, and detached scientific analysis is thereby threatened. There is clearly a danger that OR analysts would be tempted to seek the interests of the client who hired them and perhaps their vision of the high ideals of independent inquiry may become obscured. But let us face it: this danger exists with all professionals; it is certainly paramount in industrial OR groups specifically hired to look after the interests of their enterprises. Provided the analyst has the necessary convictions of professional ethics, his position on the witness stand when he testified for his client should not be essentially different from the

position of an employee working for an employer (indeed, the independence
of the former is less threatened, since he is hired to handle a single *ad hoc*
problem and is not concerned with security of employment with one particular employer).

The proposition that analysts could appear on behalf of opposing sides
has the added attraction that each will be on his mettle to ensure that his
analysis is sound and that faulty arguments have a low probability of being
unchallenged. Thus, there is a better chance than in the case of a single
analyst acting as the agent of the court that all angles of the case would be
carefully ventilated. This does not resolve the problem of the inexpert
Examiner or Judge having to rule which of the opposing professional views
is more persuasive, but such a problem faces him in other professional
spheres, when doctors, psychologists, surveyors, engineers, accountants or
economists appear as expert witnesses on opposing sides. An extension of
his judgemental abilities to examine fundamental assumptions and the logic
of conclusions in the field of quantitative model building should not be
beyond the capacity of any discerning adjudicator.

CHAPTER 12

Responsibilities of the Management Scientist

The breed of owner-managers is dying, at least in the developed countries. Most managers nowadays do not own the enterprise in which they work. They are employed by the organization, in the same way that white-collar or blue-collar workers (a somewhat antiquated distinction that still appears to be prevalent) are employed by the organization, and employee - managers experience similar uncertainties and pressures—including job insecurity —as other workers. The management scientist, too, is an employee, even when his job carries managerial status, and his future, his prosperity, and his sense of achievement are affected by the organizational environment within which he has to operate.

This raises the question of what responsibility the management scientist— and for that matter the manager too—should have towards the organization, the work force, and society at large. The fact that "we are all employees now" does not in itself eradicate the disparity between the aims of individuals or sections of the enterprise. Differences in aspirations and expectations are bound to exist, some influenced by the personal circumstances of individuals, some affected by pressures from groups to which they belong. In acting solely in the interest of the organization (essentially "the employer" in this case), the management scientist may damage the interests of groups of employees, and if he pursues certain sectional interests, the results may be detrimental to other sections or to the organization as a whole. Furthermore, what may be beneficial to the organization and/or to its employees may be undesirable for the community—local or national. How can such diverse interests be reconciled in the way the management scientist performs his job, and would he be justified in identifying himself with certain interests to the exclusion of others?

In an eloquent paper on this theme Ackoff argues that the management scientist should regard his work as a professional activity and that "professionalism clearly implies certain responsibilities to both the recipient of the professional's services and the society of which the professional is a part" [1, p. 362]. He points out that although a lawyer is employed to protect his client's interests, he is also an officer of the court and has certain obligations in that capacity. Other professionals, too, have dual responsibilities to their clients and to society: to the former in helping them to attain their goals and aspirations, to the latter in ensuring that the actions of their clients are within the law and conform to specified rules of conduct. And since such professionals (including doctors, architects, structural engineers, accountants) find it possible to operate with this dual responsibility, there appears no reason why management scientists should not.

The crux of Ackoff's argument—as he sees it—is that organizations are "purposeful systems", with "goals, objectives and frequently ideals of their own", that each system contains other purposeful systems, and that each system is in turn contained in a larger purposeful system. If this leads to conflict between a system and its parts, then it is Ackoff's contention that managers and management scientists should "learn how to remove the apparent conflict", that ways can and should be found to serve both the system and its parts, and that the management scientist's responsibility is to look after the interests of all those who can be affected by organizational decisions. By acting as an advocate for those who are not represented in the process, the management scientist can ensure that solutions are adopted to the benefit of all concerned and that the interests of the organization are served without detriment to its members. This stems from Ackoff's belief that an organization has three basic types of responsibility: to itself, to its constituent components, and to the larger system of which it is a part, and this ties in with the concept of professional conduct alluded to earlier.

Some critics launched a vitriolic attack on Ackoff for asserting that "parts of an organization have a responsibility to the whole", arguing that inmates of a concentration camp need not consider the interests of their guards, and that similarly black gold miners in South Africa only "appear to chose their employment" and cannot be expected to have a deep sense of responsibility to their employers. They then extend their proposition to apply to all workers who have no choice but "to effect the purpose of others than them-selves" [2, pp. 91 - 92]. But this is a weak argument. Firstly, as Ackoff is adamant in his retort [2, p. 96], he envisages responsibility as being mutual, of the organization to its people as well as of people to their organization, and clearly in the example of the concentration camp such mutuality of responsibility does not exist.

The assertion that the same situation pertains not only when members are forcibly held within their system, but also whenever individuals have limited freedom to choose whether to belong to a system or not has dubious validity. Admittedly gold diggers in South Africa may only appear to have a choice of employment, but so do most employees everywhere else; indeed, in some totalitarian countries, where strict manpower planning and centra-lized procedures for allocation of labour are exercised (ostensibly for the common good), even an apparent free choice for the individual does not exist. How free, then, must a choice be to qualify for exemption from the proposition of Ackoff's critics that lack of freedom absolves the individual from responsibility to the organization?

Freedom is certainly difficult to define in this context. In a free market economy (let alone one that is centrally directed) constraints are always to be found on the mobility of people from one organization to another, and while circumstances of individuals vary, factors such as family and financial commitments, skill, qualifications, experience, even age, impose severe con-straints on mobility. Some constraints are prescribed by the environment, some are self-imposed as a result of one's expectations or acquiescence with the expectations of one's immediate surroundings, so that absolute freedom rarely exists. And such constraints are not confined to any parti-cular stratum of the organizational hierarchy; even top managers often find themselves trapped in their exalted cocoons, unable to break out and choose alternative employment. To conclude that the majority of the working force—shop-floor workers and managers alike—should have no responsibility to their organization is not only a fatuous doctrine, it is a recipe for total anarchy. Ackoff's maxim that an organization has a responsibility to its members and that they have a responsibility to the organization must there-fore stand. There is no way in which organized activity involving dependence of people on each other can be sensibly construed, if it is to remain a con-structive component within a societal framework.

If this conclusion is accepted, then we come back to the question of how management scientists (and managers) should cope with the multiplicity of objectives and aspirations of the organization, the work force, and society. That conflict of interests exists between the parties concerned is manifest whenever strategic decisions of substance are taken, and it is often inevitable that actions which benefit one faction may be less beneficial, and sometimes even injurious, to others.

Such divergence of goals among the various groups affected by the decision-making process is particularly palpable when benefits and rewards are confined to short-term measures and when some groups regard long-term future benefits as so uncertain or intangible that they should be heavily discounted in favour of immediate gains.

Now, Ackoff's belief that organizations are purposeful systems, with specific goals and objectives, does not help to solve the problem. Assuming for a moment that this statement is true, we know that organizational aspirations cannot be described by a simple goal, and that when an array of performance criteria is delineated many are found to be incompatible with each other. These disparities occur even when we focus our attention on one of the interested parties—the organization—ignoring the others that may have arrays of goals of their own. The methodology available to the management scientist to deal with multiple objectives is still in its infancy, and many will argue that it cannot possibly be value-free. In this respect Ackoff is right when he states that "ethical and scientific man cannot be separated"; indeed, this applies not only to management science but to all science, and we should not be alarmed by the prospect of two management scientists coming up with different answers to the same decision problem (not because of discrepancies in their technical competence, but because of differences in their systems of values and beliefs). The notion that management scientists are "programmed devices" into which you feed data and get the "right solution" is obviously extremely naïve, even untenable, except in rather trivial cases.

But the concept of purposeful organizations is further exacerbated by the question: Who defines their purposes? An organization is not a cohesive single entity that you can go to and ask: What are your goals and aspirations? Although it has often been observed that organizations have characteristics of their own—we even talk about behaviour of (and not just in) organizations—such traits can only be discerned through the attitudes and responses of people, and it is the interpretation of these responses that provides a statement about organizational goals. Should such interrogation be confined to the top echelon—the board of directors—as the sole agents capable of seeing the "total picture", or should other echelons in the structure participate in this goal definition, and if so, how? To what extent is it conceivable that when individuals are asked about the goals of the organization their answers will not be affected by their own purposes or by group interests?

We have to conclude that either absolute organizational goals do not exist, or, if they do, that we lack the methodology that will allow them to be ascertained without bias or contamination. When it is suggested, therefore, that the task of the management scientist is to set organizational purposes against the goals of other interested parties in an effort to seek a compromise, he needs to be fully aware of the limitations inherent in such a process. Indeed, it may be argued that organizational goals are not really the goals of the organizations as such but the goals of its constituent parts. Thus, when each group or faction in the organization has its goals ascertained, they become a subset of the organizational set, which consists of all these subsets plus the perceived expectations of the rest of the community. That such a set will include many inconsistencies is, of course, inevitable, and it is the task of management—assisted by management scientists—to decide how the problem can be ameliorated and what final set should be pursued, assuming that management is prepared to be so explicit.

As for the resultant and remaining conflict of interests between the workforce, the shareholders, the customers, and the rest of society—the management scientist must accept not only that the conflict is real but that its inherent causes cannot be removed by a compromise solution. Since by definition a compromise does not give the warring factions everything they want (and, indeed, what they want is a dynamic concept in that it is constantly reviewed and adjusted in the light of what they get), it represents—if accepted by all concerned—a tolerable framework within which they are prepared to continue to collaborate, because the penalty for a collapse of the enterprise is too severe for them to contemplate, and possibly because they believe they may strike a better bargain in the next round. Thus, I find Ackoff's proposition that managers and management scientists should "learn how to remove the apparent conflict" untenable. The basic conflict cannot be removed; it can only be abated.

The real dilemma of the management scientist is whether he should confine his efforts to determining through a satisficing approach what the acceptable domain is, thereby ensuring that feasible solutions always exist and avoiding the consequences of open strife, or whether he should actively pursue a solution that he believes to be right and try to bring about its implementation. The first role is that of a skilful negotiator, the second is that of the change-agent. The first seeks to define the common ground on which a plan for action can be devised, to emphasize that there is a commonality of purpose of the various factions in the organization and that this common purpose is more important than the issues that divide them; he tries, as far as possible, not to take sides, although it is doubtful whether he can completely avoid being influenced by value and moral judgements. The second is inevitably motivated by strong convictions and he may find that he is unable to extricate himself from power politics in the organizational structure; he should then be prepared to be accused of adopting partisan doctrines, but he must maintain an adequate sense of detachment from the "client" he represents, in the same way that a doctor or lawyer has a duty to his client, and be compassionate yet remain detached, otherwise emotion may cloud his judgement and he may not be able to render the best service to his client. Both types of management scientists are needed in industry; both have a contribution to make. The role of the change-agent is less conventional and is bound to be viewed with some suspicion. It is not one which many management scientists would wish to adopt by reason of personality or conviction; it is a vitally important role nonetheless, and one that more management scientists should assume. The delineation of organizational goals in the context described earlier and the formulation of strategies that flow from such an evaluation is a task to which the management scientist should feel able and anxious to contribute. His attitude to organizational goals and their pursuance must ultimately remain a matter of professional conduct, ethical judgement, and conscience.

REFERENCES

1. Ackoff, R. L. (1974) The social responsibility of operational research, *Operational Research Quarterly*, vol. 25, pp. 361 - 71.
2. A comment and a rejoinder (1975) *Operational Research Quarterly*, vol. 26, pp. 91 - 98.

CHAPTER 13

Goals and Constraints in Decision—Making

THE NATURE OF THE PROBLEM

A well-known scientist decided that he had been a bachelor long enough, or at least that he should seriously consider whether to get married or not, and if so to whom. Being a rational man, he sat down and enumerated the advantages and disadvantages of the marital state and the kind of qualities he should look for in choosing a wife. As for the advantages—and I quote from his notes, "Children (if it please God)—constant companion (and friend in old age)—charms of music and female chit-chat." Among the disadvantages: "Terrible loss of time, if many children forced to gain one's bread; fighting about no society." But he continued, "What is the use of working without sympathy from near and dear friends? Who are near and dear friends to the old, except relatives?" And his conclusion was: "My God, it is intolerable to think of spending one's whole life like a neuter bee, working, working, and nothing after all.—No, no, won't do.—Imagine living all one's days solitarily in smoky, dirty London house—only picture to yourself a nice soft wife on a sofa, with good fire and books and music perhaps—compare this vision with the dingy reality of Great Marlboro' Street." His conclusion: "Marry, marry, marry" [5, p. 277].

Having decided that he ought to get married and having listed the desirable qualities of a future spouse, he then proceeded to look for a suitable candidate. He had several female cousins, so that there was no need to search outside the family circle. He dispassionately compared their attributes with his list of objectives and constraints, made his choice and proposed to her. Needless to say, he lived happily ever after. The scientist in question—Charles Darwin; the year—1837.

The purpose of this story is not to demonstrate that there is nothing new under the sun and that decision-making is as old as man, but to highlight the simple but systematic methodology that Darwin employed to solve a complex problem involving multiple goals. It is precisely this element of complexity which has led to so many difficulties in rationalizing the decision process: what do you do when there is no one single objective function, the value of which is a sole measure of performance or success, but when several objectives are presented and when some can be shown to be in direct conflict with others? We are all too familiar with this type of situation: we are told to increase production, reduce costs per unit, maintain quality, keep within the budget, supply the customer what he wants without delay, reduce stocks, and so on. Clearly, many of these objectives, laudable as they may be, are not compatible with each other, since they are often set in order to ensure that individual performance measures of separate departments or functions in the organization are attained. These individual measures are rarely co-ordinated adequately at the higher management echelon, and even when a serious attempt at co-ordination is made, the fundamental conflict between them is seldom eradicated.

It is this multiple goal aspect of the problem that has led to two distinct approaches to planning, the first called *optimizing* and the second *satisficing*. These concepts have been discussed by several authors [1, 3, 6], and further comments on the subject in the context of this paper would be appropriate (Table 13.1).

OPTIMIZING

Optimizing characterizes the approach of *economic man*. To solve a planning problem he prefers to define a single criterion or objective function, and he proceeds to determine such a plan that will maximize the value of this function. When presented with multiple goals, economic man resorts to one of the following methods:

(a) *Trade-offs*
The idea here is that if management is pressed hard enough and long enough, and if it is presented with repeated sets of alternative solutions between which a choice needs to be made, a system of relative values and trade-offs can be established. This would then allow specific statements to

be made as to the quantitative amount that may be sacrificed in, say, objective A, in order to attain a given increment for objective B and for management to be indifferent to the two alternative solutions involved. The result of this approach is that multiple goals are reduced, through appropriate scaling factors, to a weighted sum which represents the aggregate single objective function to be optimized.

TABLE 13.1. *Two approaches to decision making*

I. OPTIMIZING

- Single goal

- Multiple goals

    (a) Trade-offs → single weighted goal
    (b) Optimizing in tandem
    (c) Converting goals to constraints
    (d) Target setting → goal programming

II. SATISFICING

- Single goal

- Quantifiable multiple goals

    (a) Norms → a world of constraints
    (b) Interval programming

- Quantifiable and non-quantifiable goals

(b) *Optimization in Tandem*

When management refuses or is unable to provide a set of trade-offs, it may nevertheless be willing to rank the goals in some preference order A, B, C, etc. The optimizer could then proceed to determine the optimal solution with respect to A, then with respect to B, and so on. This approach assumes, of course, that after optimizing for A there is still sufficient room for manoeuvre to search for an optimal solution for B. In many cases, however, the optimal solution for A may be unique, and will automatically determine the values B, C, etc., and the problem is then reduced to one involving a single goal optimization, namely the optimization of A. To overcome this difficulty, the optimizer can explore the flexibility that may be introduced by deviating from the optimal solution of A. Thus, by sacrificing the final incremental benefit for A the solution is no longer unique and a solution may be sought that will optimize B, and a similar procedure may then be adopted for C, and so on. This approach is, in fact, a reformulation of the trade-off concept, except that instead of posing the question in the form "How much of A are you prepared to lose for a specified improvement in B?" it is stated as "What deviation from the optimum of A are you prepared to tolerate to obtain a given range or given number of solutions to allow a choice with respect to B to be made?" The difference between these two versions of the trade-off approach is a subtle one, though it may have some practical significance.

(c) *Converting Goals into Constraints*

Another method that the optimizer can adopt, in order to avoid a unique solution that simply ignores some or most of the stated goals, is to determine the minimum level of performance that would be acceptable for these goals. For example, if A is return on investment and B is sales volume and if a unique solution to maximize A implies too low a level for B, then the optimizer may ask: "What minimum level of sales must we have?" This value for B is thus described as a constraint and the problem is then solved by finding the optimal solution for A while ensuring that the constraint for B is observed.

(d) *Target Setting*

If the goals are set in the form of targets, then the difference between the actual value of a given goal and its target becomes itself a measure of performance. This difference is expressed in the form of a slack variable s_A as shown in Table 13.2, where A^* is the target compared with the actual value A. Similarly, slack variables for other goals are defined. The objective now becomes that of minimizing a function of these slack variables, e.g. their arithmetic sum, or their weighted sum (to account for different levels of importance attached to the goals or to the slacks). Another version of this approach is to differentiate between two types of slack, namely between overages (when, say, A^* is exceeded) and underages (when the target is not attained) and optimize the weighted sum, where an overage and an underage for a given goal are weighted differently. This approach is called *goal programming*, and its significant feature is that it starts with a list of goals from which an objective function is constructed. Needless to say, this function may be very sensitive to the hierarchical framework of the goals as implied by the target-setting process or by the weighting of slacks.

TABLE 13.2. *Goal programming*

Targets	A^*, B^*, C^*, etc.
Actual performance	A, B, C, etc.
Define slacks	$A + s_A = A^*$
	$B + s_B = B^*$
	.
	.
	.
Objective function	$F = s_A + s_B + \dots$
or	$F = w_A s_A + w_B s_B + \dots$

These four methods have one theme in common, namely that some form of explicit optimization of a single goal takes place. The variations on this theme are solely concerned with ways in which conflicts between goals can be resolved.

SATISFICING

Satisficing is a concept suggested by Simon [6] who propounded the theory of "bounded rationality" to describe "the behaviour of human beings who satisfice because they have not the wits to *maximize*". More specifically, if the manager finds that he is unable to reconcile conflicts between goals through the specification of trade-offs, or that he is unwilling to express all or some of his goals in the form of utility functions, then the way in which he proceeds is to determine not the best solution to a problem, but a solution that is "good enough". Thus, the planning problem of resource allocation is subjected to the need to meet certain levels of performance, such as keeping within given budgets, and attaining certain targets of profit, turnover, market share, and so on.

The question of what is "good enough" is largely answered by consensus of opinion. Each section of the organization has certain performance measures associated with its activities, and it is natural for these measures to be converted into satisficing goals. Take, for example, a sales department. Its performance is likely to be measured by such criteria as total sales volume, sales volume per employee, total costs of the department, or the ratio of sales volume to these costs. Such performance criteria, with modifications, become future targets. Last year the sales volume was V; next year it should be at least $V + \Delta V$, and if that is attained then the performance will be regarded as good enough.

Thus, in contrast to the optimizer, the satisficer is not looking for a unique solution and he makes no attempt to express explicitly how the goals are to be ranked or how conflicts between them can be resolved. There is, of course, the possibility that when all the goals have been stated, there is only one unique solution or that no solution can be found, in which case the problem has to be faced that at least some goals are too "tight" and need to be reformulated.

From a programming viewpoint there are two ways in which planning by satisficing can be undertaken, by norm setting and by interval programming.

(a) *Norm Setting*

The goals are converted into measures, which if attained are considered to be "good enough". In effect this is an extension of method I (c) in Table 13.1, except that now all the goals are converted into constraints and the problem thus becomes that of finding a *feasible solution*, or a set of solutions, to a given array of constraints. The conversion of goals into constraints is precisely what the satisficer advocates: it specifies limits which must not be violated if the solution is to be regarded as acceptable, and in that sense these newly defined constraints are not basically different from any conventional constraints. In mathematical programming terms we now have a problem with constraints but with no objective function, and the aim is to find feasible solutions and not optimal solutions. The limits defined by the new constraints are called "norms" or "standards" because in essence they describe acceptable levels of performance. Thus, I argue that in satisficing there is *no difference between goals and constraints* [3]. Essentially, all constraints are goals, since they all express desirable (or undesirable) modes of operation. If I state that in a particular situation overtime should not be used, then it is conventional to define such a statement as a constraint, but it is equally legitimate to regard such a statement as being an objective. Similarly, statements that are usually singled out as being objectives (e.g. in relation to desirable bounds of costs, profits, return on investment, job completion in specified times, and so on) may be regarded as constraints. Admittedly, constraints may differ in character and in the way that they are generated. Some are external, such as legal requirements, or conditions imposed by customers or creditors, while others are internal. Thus, not all constraints are equally inflexible or indeed equally important, and in most cases a hierarchy of constraints may be set up to reflect the order in which violation would have to progress, if need be. Perhaps the only differentiation that may be worthwhile is between the "dos" and the "don'ts". The "dos" express lower bounds of performance that must be attained (such as a minimum given level of profit or a minimum volume of sales), whereas the "don'ts" express upper bounds that must not be exceeded (such as a maximum level of costs, or a specified budget). If we were free from past conventions as to what is meant by cônstraints I would suggest that we call the "dos" objectives and the "don'ts" constraints, but with the added qualification that such a definition of objectives should not be confused with the objective function that we have become accustomed to in optimization problems in mathematical programming.

(b) *Interval Programming*

There are circumstances in which management is anxious not just to set a norm of performance in the form of a lower bound, but also to specify an upper bound. For example, the attainment of a minimum profit level may be coupled with the realization that excessive profits could become a source of embarrassment. Thus, a range—or an interval, hence the term "interval programming"—is defined and any solution that yields a level of performance within the range is considered acceptable. The specification of a constraint as an interval can be easily reformulated as two constraints, one in the form of a "do" ("do exceed the lower bound") and the other in the form of a "don't" ("don't exceed the upper bound"), and this formulation remains valid and practical provided that the two constraints are not incompatible (i.e. the upper bound must be higher than the lower bound) and that the interval is sufficiently wide to allow feasible solutions. In principle, interval programming may be regarded as an extension of norm setting, but the implications for management as to the way it proposed to approach the planning problem and design the control function may be important enough for the two methods to be listed separately.

ADAPTIVIZING

Before going any further I would like to comment briefly on the concept of *adaptivizing*, which has been suggested by Ackoff as an innovative type of planning and as distinct from optimizing and satisficing. As he puts it, "It is not prevalent today because we have neither developed a clear and comprehensive concept of it nor a systematized methodology for carrying it out. Therefore it is more an aspiration than a realization" [1, p. 15].

Ackoff continues to argue that "most of the current need for planning arises out of lack of effective management and control" and that adaptive planning "is based on the belief that the principal value of planning does not lie in the plans that it produces but in the process of producing them", so that "the value of planning to managers lies primarily in their participation in the process, not in their consumption of the product".

Cogent as these arguments may be, I find it difficult to see the justification for "adaptivizing" as a distinct mode of planning which is entirely different in concept and approach from *optimizing* and *satisficing*. Perhaps I should segregate Ackoff's arguments into the following categories and direct my comments to them accordingly:

(1) He argues that the planning process should be adaptive—as, of course, it must be, irrespective of what type it is. The optimizer and the satisficer (incidentally, it need not be a single individual in each case, and the terms equally apply to groups) must be adaptive. They need to learn from their planning process and to take account of feedback. Indeed, adaptiveness is a feature that must characterize all managerial activity.

(2) Managers must be involved in the planning process—again, this is not a maxim that anyone would quarrel with. In any study of the managerial process, whether it is associated with planning or not, the active involvement and participation of managers is essential, not only for their own edification, but for the success of the study itself and for the implementation stage when the study culminates with proposals for changes in prevailing systems. Operational researchers are so well aware of the dangers of conducting studies in isolation to the exclusion of management participation that they hardly need any convincing of this point.

(3) What is important is the process, not the product—it may be argued that, up to a point, this is the implication of all learning activities, and that management processes essentially involve learning. In that sense, Ackoff's statement about the importance of the process in relation to the product is well taken, but if he suggests that planning should be conducted not for its own sake, not in order to generate courses of action for the enterprise, but merely in order to provide a framework for managers to interact with each other, because it is "good" for them and because they can learn a great deal in this way, then why call this a planning activity? There are many other ways in which managers can be brought together and made to interact, and some may well be more effective (depending on what the precise objective of this interaction is) than the planning framework.

THE ULTIMATE AND THE FEASIBLE

To me, therefore, "adaptivizing" is a truism. It does not represent a new philosophy of planning, since I maintain that its main features of adaptation and learning must be embedded in any planning and, indeed, in any managerial activity. However, the distinction between optimizing and satisficing does represent a real divergence in approach and can usefully provide the basis of a theory of managerial behaviour. Optimizing is the science of the ultimate; satisficing is the art of the feasible. The optimizer sets off in a single-minded fashion to determine the best solution to a given problem in given circumstances, and in that sense he may be regarded as a sophisticated descendant of Taylor and Gilbreth, who were ever searching for "the one best way". The satisficer, on the other hand, acquiesces with the proposition that it is seldom possible to define the ultimate in unambiguous terms, and that it is sufficient to do "well enough" (preferably a little better than on previous occasions), namely to find a feasible solution to his problem.

As Simon remarked [6], satisficing is much more prevalent than optimizing, and the reasons are not difficult to elucidate. Apart from the problems which have already been alluded to in resolving conflicts between various desirable goals, the satisficing approach is embedded in prevailing organization structures. When an enterprise is divided into several segments, each with its own responsibilities and with criteria by which its performance and the competence of individuals are to be judged, it is only natural that such criteria inevitably become part of a multi-goal system and, furthermore, that in the management hierarchy such goals are often generated from below as a defence mechanism to counteract those generated or likely to be generated from above.

Thus, goal setting in the planning function becomes a two-way process. The higher management hierarchy has certain notions about desirable performance levels and those notions are tempered by what each segment of the enterprise argues would be possible and reasonable for it to achieve. This is how norms are set. They represent the outcome of the negotiation process, during which each segment tries to maintain as much room for manoeuvre as possible, while top management tends to "tighten" the norms as much as possible.

Notice that norms specify minimum levels of performance, which is the essence of the satisficing philosophy. If we observe closely the negotiation process that leads to norm setting, the two arguments that are often advanced are as follows:

(1) you achieved level A in the past, there is therefore no reason why you cannot achieve A (or $A + \Delta A$) in the future;

(2) plant (or company) X can achieve level A, why not you?

These arguments tend to produce norms which become "tighter" and tighter with time. I have called this elsewhere [3] *the crawling-peg phenomenon*. And since past performance, and not only competition, becomes an important element in determining norms, is it surprising that by and large managers are reluctant to optimize, or are tempted not to do too well, lest their excellent performance in one period could become the standard for the future and thereby be held against them when they fail to repeat past successes? This phenomenon has been observed often enough in the case of production workers putting a ceiling on their levels of output, or resorting to "banking" output for "lean periods", and analogous modes of behaviour are widespread amongst the managerial class.

THE PUBLIC SECTOR

I have dwelt on the optimizing and satisficing philosophies at some length in order to emphasize that the difference lies primarily in one's approach to managerial problem solving rather than in the problem area. Optimizing is a normative approach, whereas satisficing represents a theory to account for commonly prevailing behaviour and to underline the reasons that, in the circumstances described earlier, would inevitably lead to such behaviour.

This discussion is very pertinent when we turn our attention to OR in the public sector. The idea was propounded in Britain several years ago, and is mentioned even today in some circles, that we ought to design a new type of OR course in the universities devoted to the public sector. It is argued that the difference between such a course and an existing one is that the latter has developed in response to the needs of industry, where optimizing techniques play a major role, whereas orientation towards the public sector would tend to play down optimization and highlight other techniques which are thought to be more relevant to this sector. How misguided can such proposals be! To suggest that the difference between the private and public sectors lies in the fact that in the first you can and do optimize whereas in the second you cannot, is simply to ignore what happens in the real world. To be sure, goals do differ from one case to the other, not all managerial problems are alike, and models with their resultant outcomes have to be tailor-made to fit the problem and the environment for which they are designed. But the difference between problems is not necessarily or solely characterized by the fact that they belong to the private versus the public sector. Let me refer to one or two examples.

It was widely reported a few years ago that the Stationery Office (SO) in Britain had been studied by management consultants with the purpose of evaluating, amongst other things, the financial control procedures emp-- loyed. The SO is responsible for the publication and distribution of official reports commissioned by government departments and agencies, as well as official documents of Parliament, and as a government establishment it enjoys a monopolistic status in this field. In the financial year 1969/70 the SO recorded a net loss of £78,000 for a sales volume of £2.6m, and this loss was added to a cumulative loss in previous years of about £0.5m.

The fact that the consultants' report, and the details of it which were released to the press, dwelt so much on the profit and loss account is no doubt due—at least in part—to the question of whether the SO should be "hived off" to become a public corporation, and the terms of reference of the study must have affected the choice of consultants, who have a wide reputation for their accountancy practice. What I find so striking is that the main concern in this case centred on the problems of profitability and methods by which it can be enhanced, and the criteria referred to are not in any way different from those found so often in private enterprise. If you were to disguise all references to the SO it would be difficult to detect the fact that the study was directed towards a government establishment. Incidently, it is interesting that one of the observations of the report is that if the SO is "hived off" it would be able to adopt a more realistic pricing policy for its products, although why this should necessitate a change in the status of the establishment in a monopolistic situation is not at all clear. Surely, if it thought that the SO would be justified in charging more for certain services, it should be allowed to do so, irrespective of its being "hived off" or not.

Take other public services in Britain, such as London Transport, British Rail, or the Post Office. They are all concerned with providing good service, they are all sensitive to criticism in spite of or perhaps because of their monopolistic status, and they all have to reconcile their responsibilities to the public with the need to devise pricing policies that will ensure equitable pay and working conditions to their employees as well as provide adequate finance for capital expenditure. Their management problems concern the efficient use of resources and the planning of acquisition of new resources in very much the same way as in the private sector. It is naïve to suggest that British Steel and the National Coal Board—two examples of nationalized manufacturing enterprises in Britain—face problems which involve no optimization, while Imperial Chemical Industries—which is a public company— does not, or that the goals of Renault—the nationalized car manufacturer in France—were fundamentally different from those of British Leyland prior to its nationalization. To be sure, there are government and political pressures on the public sector that may prevent it from pursuing drastic policies of significant social consequences, such as plant closures resulting in widespread unemployment, and such pressures are generally more effective than those that can be brought to bear on the private sector. These differences between the public and private sectors are primarily reflected in the options that are available to management and therefore in the values that need to be assigned to the various constraints. In principle, however, both sectors follow a satisficing approach, and if in the public sector it appears at times to be more blatant, this does not in itself justify the assertion that a different type of OR is required to tackle problems in the public sector.

If we examine OR work at local authorities, we find many similarities with industrial OR: bus-routing problems, garbage collection and disposal, timetable scheduling for schools, facility location problems (schools, hospitals, ambulance services, fire stations), studies of workshop facilities and maintenance problems, costs of manpower turnover, forecasting demand for services, designing a pricing policy for swimming pools, inventory problems and purchasing. I have cited here actual studies that have been conducted by or for local authorities [see, for example, 4]. It could be argued, of course, that the main cause for the similarity with industrial OR projects stems from the fact that OR workers in the public sector have largely come from the industrial environment or have been so subjected to industrial-type OR thinking that they simply do not know any better. But the fact remains that the demand for such projects in the public sector exists, that it is well supported by those who hold the purse strings, and furthermore that positive benefits have been effected.

COST-BENEFIT ANALYSIS

Any comparison between studies in the public sector versus the private sector cannot fail to make reference to *cost-benefit analysis,* which has been hailed by many as a distinctive contribution to the evaluation of alternative solutions specifically designed for the study of problems with wide social implications. How does cost-benefit analysis relate to the goal-setting approaches discussed earlier and in what way need it be identified with the public sector?

As suggested at the beginning of this chapter, the problem of the multi-goal system is to resolve conflicts between goals, and this problem is further exacerbated when goals are measured in quite different ways or when some are initially expressed in non-quantified terms. In a search for a solution the contrast between economic arguments and social considerations becomes all too evident. The economic approach is based on the assertion that expenditures of money for the good of the community must be guided by considerations of costs and financial benefits to the community, but it does not necessarily follow that—given the choice—the community will decide to use its resources according to economic criteria. For example, economic criteria may well suggest that all central parks in London should be turned over to property developers, or that some museums should be converted to office blocks, but it is very unlikely—thank goodness—that such criteria would prevail even if the public were to be given clear and tangible evidence of the financial benefits of such schemes. Increased congestion, noise and air pollution, but in the main the loss of environmental amenities, outweigh the financial benefits, so that economic criteria become only a part of a very sophisticated array of goals in many dimensions.

What a cost-benefit analysis attempts to do is to quantify the benefits and disbenefits of any given scheme in cost terms. Perhaps the most comprehensive cost-benefit study ever undertaken was that of the Roskill Commission on the Third London Airport [2]. At the outset the Commission decided to "make use of cost-benefit analysis as the best available aid to rational decision making" [2, p. 11]. The great emphasis on cost-benefit computations and the weight they carried throughout the Commission's deliberations have attracted a great deal of criticism. As Roskill's report records, much of the criticism was levelled at three issues:

> "First, it was pointed out that some factors had been either totally omitted or only in part measured. Secondly, it was argued that the valuations themselves were wrong. To a very large extent this argument rested on the apparent disparity between the figures shown for noise and the figures shown for passenger user costs. Thirdly, it was claimed that the use of money as the common measuring rod itself introduced a distortion. One pound was worth more to a poor man than to a rich man but this was not reflected in the calculations." [2, pp. 123 - 4.]

For example, one factor that must be taken into account in the choice of an airport site is travel time and in order to convert it into monetary terms data need to be collected by observing people's behaviour and pattern of choice in order to establish a relationship between time and money. Similarly, it is argued that the adverse effect of noise on the surrounding area of the airport may be quantified in monetary values by establishing the effect of the airport on market prices and rents of houses inside and outside the noise-affected areas, as well as determining the cost of sound-proofing measures for various buildings such as schools, hospitals, or other institutions.

Another major criticism concerned the question of weighting. Once all the items to be considered are costed and benefits and disbenefits quantified in monetary terms, should they be aggregated as a simple sum or should the items be weighted to reflect their relative importance? The Roskill Commission applied no weighting and was told that no weighting is in itself a judgement of weighting [2, p. 128]. It was suggested that three aspects of weighting need to be considered: weighting for efficiency (to reflect the interests of the air traveller), weighting for equity (by considering who were the beneficiaries of the airport project and who were the losers and giving a greater weight to the latter), weighting for posterity (to account for the loss of things that the airport would destroy and which posterity would greatly value) [2, p. 128]. Indeed, the dilemma about weighting was underlined by Buchanan, who dissented from the Roskill Commission's Report. While he did not "quarrel with the principle of costing separate items in order to compare, within the conventions adopted the performance of the sites in respect of those items taken separately", he went on: "Where I begin to get into difficulties is over the aggregation of the costs to produce a 'batting order' " [2, p. 149]. The basis of his belief is that "the land of the country, after its people, is its most precious asset, not to be squandered, not to be exploited, not to be sacrificed for short term gains, but to be zealously guarded and enriched for passing on to succeeding generations" [2, p. 149]. As the Commision itself commented, such an approach regards environmental factors as *constraints*, which override all other considerations.

The parting of the ways could not be more vividly described. Reduced to its essentials, cost-benefit analysis is an attempt to convert all goals into a single monetary dimension, on the basis of which alternatives can be compared and ranked, and as we have seen this is precisely what optimization procedures are about. While cost-benefit analysis is not strictly an optimizing process, since its aim is to evaluate a given set of proposed solutions and it is conceivable that the given set does not include the optimum, the method purports to single out the best solution compared with others, and in this sense it has a great deal in common with the approach of the optimizer. On the other hand, we have the dissenting voice of the satisficer, who is not prepared to convert a multi-goal problem into a single-objective scale.

What I find so intriguing is that cost-benefit analysis should have been singled out by many as the major distinctive tool of OR in the public sector, whereas in fact cost-benefit is far less revolutionary than it is made out to be. In terms of Table 13.1 cost-benefit analysis may simply be included under the heading of "trade-offs", since this is precisely the implication of converting multi-dimensional criteria to a single dimension.

This is not to say that cost-benefit analysis is trivial and makes no contribution to a better understanding of the problems involved. But it is interesting that in the case of the Third London Airport the Government eventually decided not to accept the recommendation of the Commission in spite of a very detailed study by the Commission costing over £1m and lasting for two and a half years of hard work, aided by an able research team consisting of more than twenty people. It was the dissenting view that triumphed, that of the satisficer who put his constraints first and then looked for a feasible solution.

CONCLUSION

My contention is that, as far as the application of OR is concerned, the major difference does not lie between the public sector and the private sector, but between the optimizing and satisficing approaches to decision making. True enough, the optimizing philosophy is the one that prevails in the literature, but experience and observation suggest that satisficing is the approach that prevails in practice. There is far more to be gained from scrutinizing and ranking constraints than in constructing a super utility function to delight the heart of the optimizer. And where more so than in problems belonging to the public sector, where difficulties in defining quantitative measures and criteria are perhaps more readily understood and accepted than they are in the private sector, which has been subjected far too long to the single-minded and over-simplified notion of the profit motive?

REFERENCES

1. Ackoff, R. L. (1970) *A Concept of Corporate Planning*, Wiley.
2. Commission on the Third London Airport (1971) *Report*, HMSO.
3. Eilon, S. (1971) *Management Control*, Macmillan, London.
4. *Local Government Operational Research Unit*, Information Bulletin no. 9 (March 1971).
5. Litchfield, H. (1915) *Emma Darwin, A Century of Family Letters 1792-1896*, vol. 1, John Murray.
6. Simon, H. A. (1961) *Administrative Behavior*, Macmillan, New York.

CHAPTER 14

Mathematical Modelling for Management

INTRODUCTION

In a fascinating paper, published a few years ago, Vazsonyi considers the changing role of mathematics in the analysis of managerial problems [6]. As an example to illustrate the change in approach he cites the case of the EBQ (economic batch quantity) problem, one of the earliest and perhaps most widely quoted models in the literature of operational research. The model assumes a constant rate of demand, resulting in a saw-shaped pattern of stock level; the function of total cost per unit consists (in addition to any constant element) of two terms: one increases linearly with the batch size Q and represents the average stock-holding costs, the other declines with Q and relates to the set-up (or ordering) charge per unit. The total cost function has a minimum point Q_0, which—given the set-up cost, the holding cost, and the demand rate—can be easily determined as shown in Fig. 14.1.

This approach Vazsonyi calls "the imperative of the EBQ optimizing model. The manager must order Q_0. If he does not, he is no manager" and "he will be considered stupid, villainous, ill-mannered and odious by the lofty management scientist".

But because the EBQ model is a normative one, and because "people don't like to be told what to do", Vazsonyi presents an alternative formulation, which he calls the IF - THEN type of model. The essence of this approach is shown in Fig. 14.2, where now the model tells the manager what "excess cost" he should expect for a given deviation from the optimum Q_0, and Vazsonyi proceeds to claim that the difference between the approaches in Figs. 14.1 and 14.2 is not trivial but quite fundamental. In

119

Fig. 14.2 "the manager has a choice"; the model "does not tell him what to do", and "he may have many reasons for not ordering the quantity Q_0. (A myopic one may be that his firm does not pay for the carrying costs.)"

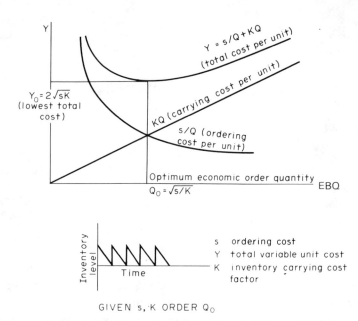

Fig. 14.1. The imperative of the EBQ optimizing model [6].

One could easily argue that there is a flaw in Vazsonyi's argument: the IF - THEN approach still relies on the same model as the optimizing - normative approach, it still clings to the cost measure as a criterion, it refers to the "excess cost" that is incurred by deviating from Q_0. The only difference is that it does not consider the deviating manager "stupid, villainous, ill-mannered and odious", and concedes that he may have his reasons, reasons which are not incorporated in the model. But the model remains normative nonetheless: it tells the manager that if he regards minimum costs per unit as imperative, he should order Q_0; if he deviates, there is a penalty (the "excess cost"). The difference between this approach and that described in Fig. 14.1 is not trivial, but it is not a fundamental one either. Figure 14.2 is still a prescriptive model because it is based on the proposition that performance should be measured on a comparative yardstick. The fact that this yardstick singles out a particular point at which no "excess cost" is incurred implies optimality and indicates a superiority (in terms of the cost criterion) of that solution over other possible solutions.

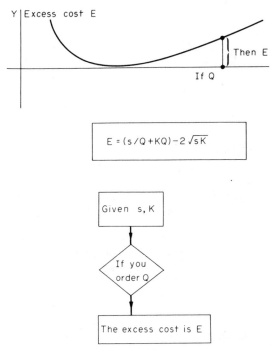

Fig. 14.2. IF-THEN (functional) model of EBQ according to Vazsonyi [6]: if Q is ordered, the excess cost is depicted.

AN ALTERNATIVE APPROACH

Several years ago I considered a somewhat different approach to this problem by suggesting the concept of the "optimal range" [1]: instead of a single optimal value Q_0 that corresponds to the mathematical optimum of the cost function, a range is specified—as shown in Fig. 14.3—within which any point is regarded as an acceptable solution. Notice that the cost model still conforms to that described in Fig. 14.1, but the difference between Fig. 14.2 and Fig. 14.3 *is* fundamental: there is no IF - THEN concept employed in Fig. 14.3, there is no "excess cost", there is no suggestion that any solution in the range is superior to any other.[1] The range acts like a tolerance specification for engineering components, which are subjected to a "go, no-go" inspection: if the dimension of a component is found to be

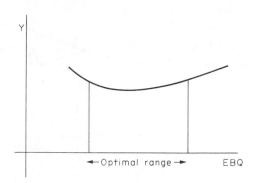

Fig. 14.3. The satisficing approach: any quantity within the specified range is equally acceptable.

within the tolerances it is accepted, otherwise the component is rejected. The question as to what tolerances to adopt depends, first, on the purpose for which the component in question is designed and, secondly, on operational considerations (e.g. the ease with which the production facilities can comply with specified tolerances). The determination of the optimal range in Fig. 14.3 may follow similar considerations, the implication being that the solution to the problem is presented in the form of bounds. The approach depicted in Fig. 14.3 exemplifies the satisficing philosophy, which is discussed at some length in the previous chapter and elsewhere [3, 4], as opposed to the optimizing approach, which is explicit in Fig. 14.1 and implicit in Fig. 14.2.

It was Lord Kelvin who suggested that "when you can measure what you are speaking about and express it in numbers, you know something about it; but when you cannot measure it, when you cannot express it in numbers, your knowledge is of a meagre and unsatisfactory kind." It is this maxim that has led to the growth of mathematical modelling in management, spurred on by efforts for increased levels of precision in the definition and solution of problems. But some believe that this process may have gone too

[1] This suggestion has not been without its critics [see 5, 2].

far, at least at the present level of understanding of the problems that managers or management scientists are faced with. The concession proposed by Vazsonyi of replacing a single imperative solution by an **IF - THEN** approach may not go far enough. We have to ask ourselves some searching questions about the applicability and scope of mathematical modelling, and about its shortcomings. It may be convenient to consider these questions under the headings of complexity, validity, accuracy, and flexibility (Fig. 14.4).

- COMPLEXITY
  > Insight through model size
  > Fear of sub-optimization

- VALIDITY
  > Appropriateness
  > Criteria
  > Horizon
  > Assumptions
  > Sensitivity

- ACCURACY
  > Relationships between variables
  > Input data (including costs)

- FLEXIBILITY
  > Room for manoeuvre
  > Need for slack

Fig. 14.4. Points to consider for the mathematical model.

COMPLEXITY

Whenever an attempt is made to model reality, the question inevitably arises as to whether the model is sufficiently elaborate to resemble the many complexities that reality presents us with. There are two schools of thought on this issue: the first claims that no model is entirely adequate and that the scientist is constantly faced with the challenge of adding and elaborating on his model to converge towards reality itself. Admittedly, this is a process with rapidly diminishing returns, but true science demands that we strive to achieve perfection, and this leads some management scientists to argue that the major weakness of our models is that they are not complex enough. In very elaborate simulation exercises this approach can result in simulation runs taking longer than real time.

The other school of thought suggests that complexity should never be pursued for its own sake, that it is rarely likely to provide new insights into the behaviour of the real system, that simple models are almost invariably preferable to complex ones. This is perhaps an extreme viewpoint; nevertheless, it is widely held by practising managers who believe that the increased complexity of models is based on increasingly dubious assumptions.

Most informed management scientists fall between the two extreme viewpoints, but inevitably some will tend towards the one more than towards the other. I confess that my sympathy lies with the latter and that the advantages for operational considerations of a simple model, in which relationships between a selected number of major variables can be easily grasped, usually outweigh the greater precision offered by a complex model. Clearly, this issue depends on the level of understanding of the problem in question. The better it is understood, the more crisply it can be defined; and the longer the managerial hierarchy has been exposed to the application of simple models, the more scope there is for further sophistication.

There is certainly a danger in complex models of glossing over some very arbitrary assumptions, which become increasingly hard to detect but whose effect on the solution may be substantial. When an analyst is faced with the task of specifying hundreds, perhaps thousands, of relationships between variables, he may be tempted to believe that each of his assumptions is not likely to be too crucial for the final outcome. And he may well be right, and often he can substantiate this belief through sensitivity analyses. But the cumulative effect of all the assumptions may well cast doubt about the structure and validity of the model as a whole.

One of the justifications for complex models is the analyst's attempt to guard against sub-optimization. For example, purchasing decisions based on inventory models concerned solely with raw materials may be very different from results of a model covering the whole purchasing - production - finished-goods - inventory system. We know, of course, that in a sense all models are sub-optimal, since any system under scrutiny is a part of a larger system. But some models are more sub-optimal than others, and it is the very narrow view taken at a single-decision centre, perhaps to the detriment of the rest of the system, that the analyst attempts to avoid.

However, one cannot help feeling some unease at the emergence of mammoth overpowering models. The hopes that size and complexity are in themselves the key to providing a better understanding of how the systems in question behave are often illusory. There is a real danger of losing sight of the wood for the trees, and the experience that many management scientists have had in this respect is sufficient to justify our concern.

VALIDITY AND ACCURACY

Validity and accuracy are closely interlinked. Validity concerns the question of the relevance of a proposed model; accuracy is associated with the quality of the information fed into the model.

Naturally, the first question that needs to be asked about any mathematical model is whether it is a valid instrument for solving a given problem. Complexity certainly impinges on validity. But there are other factors that merit consideration, such as appropriateness, the relevance of chosen criteria of performance, the assumptions adopted regarding variables and the relationships between them, and the sensitivity of the solution.

Appropriateness is undeniably a fundamental question in assessing the validity of a model to describe a given situation. Take the EBQ model, for example: it is simple to describe, it is widely quoted, it is elegant enough, and it is rarely relevant. The myopic example of Vazsonyi of a firm that does not have to pay for inventory carrying costs does not lead me to the conclusion that the approach depicted in Fig. 14.2 is then preferable to that in Fig. 14.1, but to the conclusion that the conventional EBQ model is quite inappropriate in this case. Indeed, one can argue that the EBQ model as such is often a myopic one, since it relates to an individual product or good, and if applied, for example, in a production situation the results could be quite disastrous.

And the criterion adopted by the model may also be questionable. Why do we accept as a universal truth that in inventory models the aim is to minimize costs per unit? And it is no good answering this question by saying, as many OR people often do, "well, if it is something else you want to optimize, just tell us and we'll construct the model accordingly", because tne "something else" may be just as questionable. The fact remains that in many industrial or business situations it is far from clear what single objective should be adopted. In reality, problems are rarely attuned to single objectives, and the simple-minded manipulations that are adopted through trade-offs to convert multi-objectives into a single objective are often so arbitrary as to cast serious doubts on the validity of optimization models [4].

Even the time horizon for planning models is very often in some doubt. Short-term optimization can lead to adverse consequences in the long-run, and optimization over the whole of a given horizon can be equally impeding (e.g. discounted cash flow calculations often take a dim view of long-term capital ventures and may seriously hamper technological innovation). The conflict between long-term and short-term objectives is a real one and it is not readily amenable to resolution by an optimization model.

The assumptions, too, are a serious cause for concern. We often assume in queueing models that arrival and service patterns follow stationary distributions. In reality they rarely do. We find solutions for steady state conditions, which rarely exist. We assume linear relationships to feed into LP models, or quadratic relationships in production-smoothing models to derive linear.decision rules, or probability values in decision models. In each of these cases questions of validity can be asked. Admittedly, attempts have been made to cater for dynamic situations and to incorporate more sophisticated assumptions than those described, and the literature is full of evidence of the proliferation of models to suit all tastes; but the point is that for application purposes the historical data at one's disposal are often inadequate to support the adoption of particular assumptions or particular models. I am inclined to believe that something akin to Heisenberg's principle of uncertainty applies here, namely that the greater the level of sophistication and detail with which we aspire to describe a particular situation, the greater the uncertainty associated with the results. The reason for this uncertainty lies in the difficulty in choosing the appropriate weapon to use in our ever-growing arsenal and in determining, through observation and data collection, the values of the input parameters for the chosen model.

Even the assumptions implied in measurements of costs can be crucial. How do we determine carrying costs of inventory, cost of runouts, ordering costs, set-up costs, interest charges, cost of materials and machines, fixed costs, variable costs, profit margins? Model makers tend to accept the figures they are given, but each of the items mentioned is open to several interpretations, as most accountants will readily concede.

The importance of the assumptions is clearly related to the sensitivity of the results. There is no doubt that a mathematical analysis of sensitivity can make a very useful contribution to the modeller in concentrating on the crucial parts of the model rather than on marginal frills, to the data collector in designing his data retrieval or sampling procedures, to the manager in segregating major and minor decision variables. For example, the fact that reorder quantities in inventory models are sensitive to mean demand but relatively insensitive to the standard deviation of demand or to the shape of the distribution, has important practical implications on the amount of time and effort required to ascertain the demand characteristics. But the attitude of management scientists to sensitivity is bound to be ambivalent: on the one hand, they like insensitive and robust models, yielding solutions that are not too dependent on the accuracy and interpretation of cost data and other assumptions. But when the model becomes so insensitive that it yields the same result irrespective of what you feed into it, its usefulness vanishes. This is a dilemma that merits perhaps more attention than it has apparently attracted.

FLEXIBILITY

Finally, we have to ask whether the results of the model leave any room for manoeuvre in the decision process and what new problems are thereby created. If the model leads to a single inevitable prescription, the manager ceases to exercise his managerial role with respect to the decision in question, since he is no longer free to make a decision—the model has done it for him. And room for manoeuvre is only partly tolerated by the IF - THEN approach. Flexibility can be better provided by generating bounds within which managers are entirely free to make choices, as implied by the satisficing approach [4].[2]

In an LP model with a single objective function, for example, the optimal solution usually lies at a vertex point which is defined by the

[2] See Chapter 13.

intersection of two constraints. At that point, two resources are used to
the maximum. However, for operational reasons it may be far better to
adopt a solution on a face of the multi-constraint polygon, where only one
facility•is employed to the maximum, and devote managerial effort to that
facility rather than have to ensure that two are fully utilized. Whether one
could go as far as to say to the manager that he can choose any point on
that face of the polygon in question obviously depends on circumstances.
But the principle that it is preferable to give him some freedom of choice
rather than confine him to a single prescribed solution is one that should
be more widely considered. Prescription may have its attractions to top
management in that it tends to result in a consistent and predictable performance, but prescription leads to the enhancement of the bureaucratic
process, which may stifle individual initiative and flair. Furthermore,
systems need a certain amount of slack to cater for the unexpected and
for the unprogrammable.

CONCLUSION

Mathematical modelling has made an immense contribution to management—it has helped to convert muddled thinking and amorphous deliberations into an orderly analysis, allowing crucial issues to be highlighted and
purposely debated. It has taken the mystique out of some managerial
tasks. It has allowed for many programmable decisions to be programmed
and has shown how certain analytical tools cut across conventional bound-
aries between types of managerial functions, or even industries.

But the present shortcomings of mathematical modelling and the blind
belief of some modellers in the infinite power of mathematical analysis
have led to a backlash. The criticisms range from accusations that most
analysts address themselves to the wrong problems, to suggestions that
analytical models are inappropriate for solving managerial problems. It is
important for us to recognize the various shortcomings and limitations of
the present state of the art in order to appreciate the true contribution
that can be made in order to combat the total rejection advocated by a
growing number of sceptics.

REFERENCES

1. Eilon, S. (1960) A note on the optimal range, *Management Science*, vol. 7, no. 1, pp. 56 - 61.
2. Eilon, S. (1964) Dragons in pursuit of the EBQ, *Operational Research Quarterly*, vol. 15, no. 4, pp. 347 - 54.
3. Eilon, S. (1971) *Management Control*, Macmillan.
4. Eilon, S. (1972) Goals and constraints in decision making, *Operational Research Quarterly*, vol. 23, no. 1, pp. 3 - 15; also, in Chapter 13 of this book.
5. Tate, T. B. (1964) In defence of economic batch quantity, *Operational Research Quarterly*, vol. 15, no. 4, pp. 329-40.
6. Vazsonyi, A. (1973) Why should the management scientists grapple with information systems? *Interfaces– The Bulletin of the Institute of Management Sciences*, vol. 3, no. 2, pp. 1 - 18.

CHAPTER 15

The Elusive Yardstick

Evaluation of corporate performance, like the philosophers' stone, has been the object of a persistent search by man—the ultimate yardstick by which to measure and pass judgement about the progress of an industrial enterprise. Measurement of performance is essential for all managerial activities to be at all meaningful—without it, it is impossible to set unambiguous targets, to engage in useful planning exercises, to state whether plans have been properly executed, to compare two enterprises in the same industry.

And this is why so much attention has been devoted by writers and practitioners to the problems of defining performance criteria. At the tactical level, with which lower and middle management is closely concerned, there are many facets of performance which seem relatively simple to measure: it is possible, for example, to state that production output or sales in a given week was X whereas the target was Y, or that expenditure was E compared with a budget B; it is, similarly, possible to record man-hours per unit product made, downtime of machinery and plant, number of defective components for each production facility, and studiously to compare the figures with earlier periods to detect improvement or deterioration. And on the financial side there is a multitude of criteria, based on balance sheets, cost or profit centres, and financial ratios of various kinds to help in the analysis. But all these criteria are subject to various interpretations, to methods of measuring assets and liabilities, to valuations of resources (do you, for example, value your finished goods inventory as raw materials, as materials plus labour and perhaps other costs, or as suggested by the selling price?), to alternative ways of depreciating plant and machinery, to mention but a few of the many factors involved.

Thus, costs and profits may be regarded as a convention, reflecting a particular method or approach, and as such they may be, to some extent, quite arbitrary. Readers will be familiar with many examples of accountants and professional advisers giving contrasting views on the same set of accounts. But even when the method of measurement is not in dispute and when performance is to be based entirely on the degree to which predetermined targets are attained, questions often arise as to how these targets are set in the first place. Achieving an easy target in one case and falling short of an unrealistic one in another should not necessarily be interpreted as success in the former and failure in the latter.

Add to these quantitative areas of corporate endeavour, which are at least described by numbers and are therefore seemingly unambiguous, evaluations of a qualitative nature, such as the effectiveness of the organizational structure, or the decision-making processes or the recruiting policy, or morale, and the enormity of the evaluation task begins to emerge.

It is against this background of complexity that I began to examine the six volumes by Blake and Mouton entitled *How to assess the Strengths and Weaknesses of a Business Enterprise* [1] ; the first five are devoted to the prominent functional areas: operations, marketing and sales, research and development, personnel management, financial management; the sixth volume is about corporate leadership.

If I expected a highly prescriptive "do-it-yourself" manual, I was not disappointed. The collection is, in fact, sub-titled *Organization diagnostic 6-pak*, it is offered as "one means of arriving at a total corporate health assessment" and "is written in such a way that it can be applied throughout an organization, from the presidential office downward, to make a total corporate diagnosis".

The proposed diagnostic analysis is related to three dimensions. The first covers the six *areas* listed earlier (operations, marketing and sales, etc., the sixth being corporate leadership). The second dimension is called *perspectives* and is related to three rubrics: *current effectiveness* ("the caliber of present behavior, performance and results"), *flexibility* ("the ability of the company to shift swiftly and surefootedly to meet unanticipated changes of a short term character"), and *development* (which deals "with long term strategies which, if well formulated, increase the likelihood of the business being able to achieve profitable growth in the extended future"). The third dimension, called *orientations,* deals with the evaluation of each

of the 18 cells so far identified (=6 areas × 3 perspectives), whose actions
are to be "classified as either *internal* or *external* in scope, and as either
aggressive or *defensive* in purpose", so that four combinations of these two
orientations emerge: *internal aggressive* (efforts directed to the better use
of men, money, machines, and materials), *internal defensive* (concern with
"internal weakness of behavior, performance and results"), *external aggressive*
(assessment of how the enterprise takes advantage of opportunities in the external environment) and, *external defensive* (awareness of the actions of
competitors and other external forces).

A list of issues in each area is then given and a scale of performance is
specified in which the rating 9 denotes corporate excellence regarding an
issue under scrutiny whereas the rating 1 represents failure to approach
satisfactory performance by a wide margin. Thus, assessing performance
in this way with respect to the issues listed provides an overall picture of
corporate posture and behaviour in various areas. Blake and Mouton argue
that "this instrument is not a test, but provides a managerial road map for
evaluating where your area's performance is presently located, in relation
to standards of excellence as defined by experts of management. A reader
will be able to rate his business enterprise on a number of different factors,
and these judgements will be useful in a diagnostic way."

But their insistence that this exercise is a "diagnosis, not measurement"
is impossible to sustain. How can you draw a road map without measurement? How can you mark performance on a hierarchical scale without testing and comparing corporate activities with bench marks on the predefined
scale, and if that is not measurement—what is?

The problem can perhaps be best illustrated by an example. Take the
area of operations in which the very first issue discussed is *productivity*
("output expressed in terms of effort or expense" and "may be evaluated
in units per man-hour or man-days, equipment utilization, cost per unit, or
in continuous flow operations in cost of throughput") which is to be marked
on the following scale:

9 completely effective (maximum productivity is realized at minimum
   expense)
8 almost completely effective
7 quite effective
6 moderately effective
5 as effective as ineffective ("satisfactory but less than should be

realized for the level of expense incurred; significant improvements in productivity are possible")

4 moderately ineffective

3 quite ineffective

2 almost completely ineffective

1 completely ineffective ("productivity is excessively low or so costly as to result in a marginal or loss operation")

This is a typical scale which is used throughout for all the other issues raised in the diagnostic exercise, and there are no less than 320 issues for the 6 areas listed earlier; of these, 53 issues are devoted to the operations area (and many are repeated for the other areas): 19 on "current effectiveness" (subdivided into 11 on "internal aggressive", 5 on "internal defensive", 1 on "external aggressive", and 2 on "external defensive"), 20 on "flexibility", and 14 on "development" (again both "flexibility" and "development" are subdivided each into the four "windows" of internal/external and aggressive/defensive combinations).

Whether the issues listed by Blake and Mouton for each area are the most appropriate or the most relevant for all enterprises is very much in doubt: in one firm the problem of centrally finished product inventory may be crucial; in another product design or methods of manufacture may be of prime concern. Some firms may have problems which are not directly covered by the authors' elaborate list of issues, whereas other firms may be advised to concentrate only on some of the listed issues and ignore most of the others. Furthermore, it is very doubtful whether the same set of issues for a given firm is appropriate for all levels in the organizational hierarchy. To suggest that the same diagnostic tool-kit can be used "throughout an organization, from the presidential office downward" is obviously a gross oversimplification of the type of measures and analyses required at each level.

If the authors intend their list of issues merely as a general framework for debate on corporate performance, allowing flexibility in determining which issues are appropriate and how they should be defined, then the exercise is certainly a laudable one. In that case the actual rating for any particular issue is less important than the discussion on corporate strengths and weaknesses with respect to that issue; indeed, the numerical rating is unnecessary. I say this not only because I feel that the proposed rating is very imprecise, indeed arbitrary, but because its alleged precision can divert attention from a qualitative analysis which may be more fruitful. Some may argue that a rating is nevertheless useful, that in examining such an issue as "communication within management" (one of the issues listed), one may well be subjective in one's judgement, but it is no more precise or imprecise than marking a student's essay on some chosen aspects of, say, the English novel. In fact, it may be easier to rate "communications within management" than "productivity", since the former would be readily recognized as being an impressionistic evaluation, whereas the latter has a misleading aura of precision, misleading because in most firms it is far from clear how productivity should be measured and compared.

Some of the listed issues are singularly vague in their description or relevance: the "concept of synergy", for example, is undoubtedly important for various industrial enterprises, but rating 9 (associated with "complete flexibility") is to be given when "decisions are viewed in the light of this concept in ways that result in significant multiplier effect in terms of both profit improvement and expense reduction". Many readers attempting to apply Blake and Mouton's diagnostic exercise to their firms will find such definitions quite amorphous and unhelpful.

There are issues for which the authors' value judgement in the rating scheme is blatantly biased. Take the "use of consultants", where rating 9 is given when "arrangements for consultation permit competence to be applied in the solution of problems in a timely and expense conscious way; good understanding exists within the company of the skills and limitations of consultants in a variety of fields of competence". This is contrasted with the "use of consultants is not permitted" at the bottom end of the scale with rating 1. It is very arguable that this attitude as to whether a firm should or should not employ consultants is universally held.

However, as long as the list of issues serves to stimulate questions about corporate performance, and as long as the exercise is carried out in a tactful and constructive way, it can only be for the good. Where one cannot help but cringe is at any suggestion that the various ratings given on the individual issues should be in some way combined, added up, or averaged, to provide a global measure of performance. But this is precisely what the authors do suggest in a section entitled "How close to excellence?" The reader is carefully instructed to find the average score for "current effectiveness", for "flexibility", and for "development", needless to say with separate scores in each of these categories for "internal", "external", "aggressive", and "defensive", and a grand average score for the operations area as a whole. The process is repeated at the end of each volume for all the other areas. And, finally, the inevitable corporate grand average is to be calculated as the sum of the area grand averages divided by 6 (the number of areas considered).

Clearly, it matters less what you calculate than how you interpret the result, and the authors have some sensible advice to offer in that respect, particularly focusing the attention of the reader on the areas or issues for which he feels responsible. But one remains completely baffled by the naïvity of the mechanistic and utterly futile rating schemes and by the obsession with the possible significance of the area of the corporate grand score.

This is a typical example of an attempt to convert a multi-dimensional goal system into a single weighted objective function, except that in this case the individual scores are added without weighting, thereby suggesting that all the issues listed have equal weighting. This is patently unrealistic, but any elaborate system of weighting that aims at equating a given level of attainment in one dimension with a level of attainment in another is not only fraught with innumerable methodological difficulties, but is unlikely to gain universal acceptance, at least not with our present state of understanding of value systems. Thus, the introduction of a weighting structure into Blake and Mouton's diagnostic scheme is not likely to be fruitful and will not satisfy critics of this gallant but futile attempt to produce a performance index. Alas, a single yardstick for measuring corporate performance remains elusive as ever.

REFERENCE

1. Blake, R. R. and Mouton, J. S. (1972) *How to assess the Strengths and Weaknesses of a Business Enterprise*, Scientific Methods Inc., Texas.

CHAPTER 16

Seven Faces of Research

One often hears arguments about research in the field of management: What is its purpose? Is it to make us understand better the kind of problems that managers have to face? Is it to provide us with sharper predictive tools about the behaviour of people, markets, and manufacturing systems? Is it to make us better decision-makers?

And who should be conducting research in this field? The manager (or his agent), who is immersed in the environment to be studied, or an objective outsider who has no axe to grind? And what should the research report consist of? Just a statement of fact, or also an evaluation and perhaps even a prescription for future action?

While these questions can be directed to research activities in any field of human endeavour, they are perhaps more pertinent and more difficult to resolve in the field of management than, say, in the pure sciences. Since research in management often impinges on several disciplines, research techniques (and indeed attitudes as to how it should be conducted) are likely to vary, and arguments about the validity of a particular research approach are bound to ensue.

At the risk of oversimplifying the issues involved, I suggest that there are seven archetypes of research workers, which for convenience I shall call the *chronicler,* the *dialectician,* the *puzzle-solver,* the *empiricist,* the *classifier,* the *iconoclast*, and the *change-agent*. In practice we find, of course, that research workers are (sometimes inadvertently) a bit of each, but the archetypes may help us to discern between fundamentally different approaches to research in this field.

THE CHRONICLER

The Chronicler regards himself as the true detached observer. He may also be called an anthropologist, or a photographer. His function is to record for posterity a series of facts or a pattern of behaviour, so that people can turn subsequently to a record and establish what events have taken place at a particular time. He may be regarded as a photographer in the sense that he records a snap-shot (or a film) of reality, and being an outsider he takes pains to ensure that his presence does not distort in any way the course of events under scrutiny. Similarly, the anthropologist is anxious to study tribal customs and behaviour as a detached observer. The chronicler in the management field will see it as his duty to follow similar rules by devising data-collection techniques that in themselves do not interfere with reality, or are thought to have such a minimal effect on the environment as not to disqualify his findings from being a true record of events.

The chronicler need not, of course, confine himself to the data-collection activity. He may feel compelled to interpret and comment on the results of his observations, just as research workers do in the physical sciences. If his interpretations are anathema to another scientist, the latter could take issue with the conclusions and make comments of his own. This process is facilitated by the research report making a clear distinction between facts and opinion, so that anyone wishing to examine the facts on their own, without having to accept the analysis and conclusions of the original researcher, is able to do so.

This oversimplification cannot be allowed to pass without some important qualifications. For one thing, it has been argued that the true, unbiased, detached and objective observer does not exist. In reality there is a plethora of facts and it is just not possible to record them all. And so a selection has to be made, presumably of "significant" (as opposed to trivial) facts, but this entails a judgement as to which facts are important and which are not. Like a photograph, taken at a particular angle and focused in a certain way, any record of past or current events is a reflection of the particular emphasis which the observer has chosen to give it.

Another reason for the dubious validity of the concept of the completely unbiased observer lies in the proposition that the scientific method requires the researcher to have a theory or hypothesis which he intends to test when he embarks upon a data-collection exercise. Believers in the hypo-thetico-deductive method of science will naturally expect the researcher to have certain views and attitudes towards the problem under study, and indeed certain expectations of the outcome of his investigation. Thus, two chroniclers recording the same reality may not come up with identical versions of a series of events, in the same way that two photographers sent to the same scene may well produce two versions of what they see. We find this phenomenon in everyday experience. Take a meeting between two people and ask them to record the gist of their conversation, and you often find outstanding differences in emphasis and interpretation of what has been said; you sometimes wonder whether the two have in fact attended the same meeting.

A record of events is the product of the perception of the observer. It is because he has to make choices of what and how to record, and because these choices are likely to be affected by personality and attitudes, that the final outcome cannot be regarded as absolute or definitive. In practice, therefore, it is not only the conclusions of one researcher that can be challenged by another, but the "bare facts" as well, and the manner of their collection.

Another real problem encountered in research in the management field is the ability of the observer to avoid influencing the environment under study. Research workers in the social sciences are well aware of this prob-lem: if we send people questionnaires, or subject them to interviews, or just place a tape-recorder in front of them to record what they say—can we be absolutely certain that the behaviour and response of the people con-cerned remains thereby unaffected? Answering a questionnaire, or parti-cipating in an interview, may well contribute to the formation of views and attitudes which are then expressed as results of the data-collection exercise, but to what extent did such facts exist prior to the exercise? And this "observer effect", as it has come to be called, is not necessarily one that needs to be attributed to the possible way in which the observer formu-lated his questions and the possible nuances that his own attitude or behaviour may cause a biased response, but merely to the fact that when a measuring instrument is placed in a system to measure certain character-istics of a given phenomenon, its very presence affects the system and the phenomenon in question.

THE DIALECTICIAN

Whether he succeeds in his aspirations or not, the chronicler strives to remain detached from the system under observation. If possible, he would prefer his data-collection exercise to leave no trace in the system, and where the awareness of his existence as an observer is inevitable, he is at pains to ensure that his presence is as innocuous as possible.

The dialectician takes a different stance. Like the chronicler he aims at objectivity, but he believes that in human affairs it is necessary to debate and argue issues in order to elicit the facts. The chronicler aims at keeping the system undisturbed; the dialectician feels compelled to un-settle it, by challenging stated views or records, in order to uncover what otherwise may remain hidden from an innocent observer.

That the dialectician's interaction with the system is likely to distort the record or that it may inadvertently have a permanent residual effect on the system, long after the researcher has left, is perhaps inevitable. These are risks that the dialectician is prepared to take for the sake of attaining his own perception of the facts. That he can remain truly objective through-out the exercise is doubtful, although his intention is to keep his dialectic intervention entirely divorced from a missionary or a therapeutic role (which typifies the approach of the change-agent to be discussed later). Any residual effects that remain or evolve after the departure of the dialectician are manifestations of the learning process injected into the system by the dialectic methodology, and these are effects which the dialectician is prepared to accept.

THE PUZZLE-SOLVER

The puzzle-solver is a very different kind of research worker from the chronicler or the dialectician. He is much less concerned with the mecha-nics and intricacies of data collection than with the intellectual activity associated with solving a well-structured problem. I call him a *puzzle-solver* rather than a *problem-solver,* because the latter does carry the con-notation of having first to define the problem and its objectives. The puzzle-solver is happy to accept the definition and the objectives set by someone else, as for example in the case of mathematical or chess prob-lems. The configuration is given, the rules of what is allowed or is not allowed are prescribed; the problem is to find a solution that satisfies pre-defined conditions: prove a certain relationship, compute the value of a certain variable, find the best strategy (to win a game, to maximize return, to minimize costs).

The true puzzle-solver does not see it as his function to question whether he is solving the right problem. When faced with a chess problem his reaction is not "this is a ridiculous situation that no decent chess player would allow himself to get into, hence the problem is not valid"; he accepts that the situation has arisen (hiding any disdain he may feel towards the chess player in question) and proceeds to evaluate the best moves that each player can make with the object of winning the game.

This clear line of demarcation between the problem-definer and the puzzle-solver absolves the latter from responsibility of data collection and from the need to have close interactions with the environment in which the alleged problem has arisen. He is not even concerned with whether he is tackling the right problem, or whether it is an important or trivial problem in its environmental context. For the puzzle-solver a trivial problem is one for which methods or solutions are straightforward or well known, while a difficult problem is one that presents an intellectual challenge of some substance, although the economic or managerial consequences of the former may well outweigh the possible benefit accruing from a solution to the latter.

The attraction of puzzle solving is that it provides an opportunity to delve into the realm of abstraction. A particular problem may be generalized, new classes of problems may be formulated, and the analysis of the investigator may attain an intellectual value and even elegance of its own, unadulterated by ambiguous or contentious interpretations of facts gathered from *ad hoc* situations. And it is because he is largely concerned with the search-for-solution (once the problem has been defined) that the puzzle-solver is often regarded by others as a mere technician, although this is not a description that many puzzle-solvers will necessarily consider derogatory.

Operational researchers are sometimes justifiably accused of being puzzle-solvers. Indeed, there are some who argue that OR (operational research) is just a branch of applied mathematics, and that OR men delight in abstraction and abhor reality (their credo being: "*if* A is your problem, *then* B is your solution; I take pride in the latter, but no responsibility for the former"). But this may be too harsh. There are many OR men who do get actively immersed in problem definition and who indeed see it as the more taxing part of their function compared with the puzzle-solving exercise. One may perhaps regard such an OR man as merely a mixture of the three types of research workers discussed so far, although some OR workers clearly exhibit traits which belong to other archetypes.

THE EMPIRICIST

Physicists, chemists, biologists, and engineers (amongst others) have a long tradition of empirical research, relying on observation and experiment. The purpose of designing experiments is clearly to create new sets of conditions for a system under observation in order to determine the validity or otherwise of certain hypotheses. The results of such experiments either enhance the confidence of the researcher in current theories or lead him to make new propositions about the behaviour of the system and the relationships between its various parameters. In short, experimentation is intended to provide a better understanding of entities and phenomena under scrutiny.

In management science there is, alas, only limited room for experimentation, particularly when large-scale changes to the system or the environment are contemplated. Simulations, pilot plants, market trials, organizational changes—all these are experiments of a kind, but because the industrial enterprise interacts with the outside world and is constantly subjected to the impact of many exogenous variables, controlled experiments as understood by the pure scientist or engineer are difficult, often impossible, to conduct.

Many scientific experiments under laboratory conditions are carried out with the object of investigating the effect of variables when they assume extreme values. Wide variations allow stability and robustness to be examined in order to identify conditions under which a given system is likely to perform unsatisfactorily or to fail, so that such conditions can be avoided in normal operating circumstances. Experimentation of this kind can also help to compare performance under alternative conditions and to determine their preferred values. But in the study of industrial organizations such experiments are just too risky, since they may jeopardize the well-being of the system, and perhaps even its survival. This means that apart from simulation studies, experimentation in management science is largely confined to minor changes in the system, or to comparative studies of systems which have certain similarities and certain differences, in order to establish the effect of such changes or differences.

The main problem facing the researcher in such studies is that of causal attribution. If a system is subjected by design to specified changes in its operating conditions and is observed over a period of time, may one attribute any perceived changes in system behaviour to the premeditated changes or to other causes? Since over a period of time the researcher rarely enjoys the luxury of maintaining the system under steady state conditions, there is always some doubt as to whether the real causal relationships have been, or can be, established.

THE CLASSIFIER

Another type of research worker does not concern himself with the collection of information, but with the organization and categorization of data that have already been gathered, and—when appropriate—with projections that can be made as a result. This is *the classifier*. To perform his task, he needs to produce definitions that specify the commonality of attributes of members of a given class (such as entities, data, events, phenomena), as well as the distinction between members of different classes. This involves an understanding, or a proposed explanation, of the underlying factors that determine the similarities and differences in question, and explicitly or implicitly this means that the classifier has a hypothesis about the behaviour of the system under study.

As the classifier is not involved in data collection, either as a chronicler or as an empiricist, he relies on the findings of others, and inevitably he will put his own interpretation on such findings and be selective in what he considers relevant to his deliberations. As he sifts through the data, a pattern develops in his mind, emerging in a classification of the data embedded in a model or a hypothesis about relationships between key variables, thus bringing order and structure to bear on the data.

There are, however, numerous occasions when the information at his disposal is rather scanty, and the classifier is then left with his own perception of reality, bolstered perhaps by his past personal experience in a managerial context, as the basis on which to construct his theoretical framework. In principle, he remains a classifier, and the many examples of postulates in the field of organization behaviour may be regarded as classification exercises. That in such circumstances the classifier is an inductivist is inevitable, since it is often in the nature of the classifier to generalize from the particular.

What the classifier has in common with the chronicler, the dialectician, and the empiricist, is that they all strive to construct a model of reality, but while the other three are very much concerned—each in his own way—with ascertaining what the facts are, the classifier does not see himself in the role of an observer or experimenter, but as a contributor to the post-information-gathering stage. His strength stems from his ability to detach himself from the detailed intricacies of measurement activities and to be free from their possible subjective influences; his weakness lies in a perception of reality which at times lacks an intimate understanding of the information at his disposal, and which may be based on arbitrary selectiveness of information during the classification and modelling process.

THE ICONOCLAST

One effective way of conducting research is to challenge current thinking and theories. This is the role of *the iconoclast*, the breaker of cherished beliefs. He bases his challenge on one or more of the following arguments:

- current beliefs are associated with doubtful or arbitrary assumptions
- the reasoning that follows the assumptions is not sufficiently rigorous
- the conclusions are too general to be applied in specific cases, or too narrow to allow adequate generalization
- these conclusions or beliefs involve certain inconsistencies which may cast doubt on their validity
- there is incompatibility between theory and practice, as illustrated by empirical evidence.

All these arguments are based to some extent on value judgements, and what may seem to one authority a compelling reason for abandoning a given theory, may be regarded by others as totally inadequate, particularly when the theory in question can be flexibly interpreted or modified in a relatively minor way to take account of the objections raised. Interpretation, and rigorous definitions, very often become crucial in such cases, and reactions to the iconoclast often take the form of a semantic debate, as one can see in many examples in the field of organization theory, or in the analysis of criteria for evaluating the performance of an enterprise.

The iconoclast need not confine himself to the role of a critic, and his attempts to demolish existing beliefs may well be followed by alternative theories that he may wish to propose. But there are some research workers who are content to remain iconoclasts and who see their challenge to accepted fundamentals not as a destructive act, but as an important and necessary contribution that would free their colleagues from the shackles of entrenched conventions and would encourage them to take a fresh look at whatever evidence is thought appropriate.

THE CHANGE-AGENT

All the archetypes discussed so far, with the exception of the puzzle-solver, are concerned with establishing facts and theories of behaviour. Some approach their task by devoting their efforts to fieldwork, as observers or as experimentalists; others confine themselves to theoretical deliberations and attempt to make various generalizations. But whether the subject matter under study is a particular case or a class of systems, they have a common objective as an end product: a model that describes reality and can provide a basis for propositions on causal relationships, ultimately in a form that would allow the model to be used for predictive purposes. The only exceptions are the extreme chronicler, who records events but assiduously refrains from commenting on them or from interpreting the record, and the puzzle-solver, who is concerned with finding a solution to a specified problem in an abstract fashion, irrespective of whether the problem bears any resemblance to a real situation or not.

Furthermore, the six archetypes' main aim is to increase their knowledge and understanding of a given system, not to change it. Of the six only two —the dialectician and the empiricist—interact with the system; the other four strive to remain detached and hope that the observer-effect will be minimal or even immaterial. And the deliberate interactions that the dialectician and the empiricist get involved in are solely with the object of eliciting further information, again with the hope that the observer's effect will rapidly decay, although with administrative systems such expectations are often questionable, particularly after the intervention of the dialectician.

The seventh archetype is *the change-agent*, whose prime objective is to change a given system, not by merely studying it and proposing in a consulting role how it could be altered, but by being part of the system (at least for a while) and helping to change it from within. Unlike the dialectician, the change-agent debates issues with members of the system not just with the object of everyone concerned (including the investigator) gaining a better understanding of its structure, but with the view of influencing their attitude and their mode of operation, even with the intention of changing the structure and organization of the system.

There are two types of change-agents. The first acts as *a catalyst*: he is careful not to impose his views or to challenge current procedures and constraints in a blatant fashion. His aim is to assist members of the enterprise to define "the real problems" facing them and to evolve solutions (preferably his own) for change. The second type is *the activist*, who not only has views as to what goals and solutions the system needs to adopt, but takes action to steer the system towards them, by making explicit proposals, by arguing the advantages of his solutions, even by participating in the responsibility for implementation.

Two serious questions need to be asked about the change-agent: one is on the question of ethics, the other is whether his role falls into the realm of research. The ethical problem relates to the right of the change-agent to intervene and alter the system. On what ethical grounds can he assume such a responsibility under the guise of a research worker? This problem does not arise in the case of the management consultant, who acts within agreed terms of reference and who is pledged to look after the interests of his client. But the change-agent has no such agreed framework. His ideas, perceptions of the problems and remedies evolve as he pursues his investigations; he has no clients nor predetermined interests to defend, unless he argues that he is concerned with the interests of the enterprise as a whole (a statement that begs several questions). Is it appropriate, or justifiable, for him to seek to influence the system to adopt certain courses of action?

This issue is discussed further elsewhere,[1] and it is obviously a matter of judgement and conviction. Management scientists who see themselves as agents of change will take the view that such an intervention is perfectly legitimate, even when two change-agents in a given situation may not agree on what prescribed solutions the enterprise should adopt.

But the question of whether the change-agent may be regarded as a research worker remains. Those who believe that the purpose of research in management science is "to identify, extend and unify scientific knowledge pertaining to management"[2] may regard the change-agent with the utmost suspicion, while on his part he may argue that his *investigation*

[1] See Chapter 12.
[2] A definition adopted by the Institute of Management Sciences.

methodology is not drastically different from that of the dialectician, and that any adjustments that are incorporated in the system give him even greater opportunities to study the empirical effects of change.

CONCLUSION

Categorizing research workers as I have done (assuming here the role of a classifier) is not to suggest that individuals can be easily put in well-defined compartments. It has been pointed out earlier that some research workers combine several attributes and are not content to be identified with any single approach. Also, it is possible for a given investigator to act in different roles in different circumstances: as a chronicler in one study, as a classifier in another, and as an empiricist in a third. But one finds that many researchers are committed to a particular school of thought or methodology, either because it has affinity with the academic discipline from which they have originally come, or because of a combination of habit and conviction. It is very often the lack of understanding of the precise nature of each archetype that generates a great deal of criticism and cynicism, some of which is undoubtedly justified, but some embedded in prejudice. Each archetype has a contribution to make, but each suffers from certain limitations and weaknesses that sometimes assume magnified proportions in *ad hoc* circumstances, with implications on the ability to generalize and advance our knowledge in the field of management science. One hopes that an informal debate on the strengths and shortcomings of alternative approaches to research and their underlying attitudes and philosophies will prove to be profitable.

CHAPTER 17

How Scientific is OR?

"Operational Research is the application of the methods of science to complex problems arising in the direction and management of large systems of men, machines, materials, and money in industry, business, and defence. The distinctive approach is to develop a scientific model of the system, incorporating measurements of factors such as chance and risk, with which to predict and compare the outcomes of alternative decisions, strategies or controls. The purpose is to help management determine its policy and actions scientifically."

This is the official definition of OR (Operational Research) adopted by the OR Society in Britain, and the definition is prominently displayed on the first page of every issue of the *Operational Research Quarterly*. The word "science" or its derivatives "scientific", and "scientifically" appears three times in this statement, and in its recent search for a new and perhaps more concise definition, the Society has been offered numerous alternatives which similarly seek to emphasize the scientific nature of the OR activity. The term Management Science (which some identify as synonymous with OR, and others regard as more broadly based) has even "science" in its title; the "application of the scientific method" is repeatedly asserted in the many texts on OR published in recent years.

It is, therefore, proper to ask whether such claims are justified and to explore the extent to which OR may or may not be regarded as scientific in character. But before we do this, it is necessary to describe briefly the nature of scientific inquiry, or at least one particular view of it.

THE SCIENTIFIC METHOD

Taking a leaf from the well-known definition that "economics is what economists do", one may be tempted to say frivolously that "science is what scientists do", but this is not likely to satisfy our curiosity. Medawar considers two conceptions of science. The first is that of an overriding concern with factual knowledge, a concept that he totally rejects: "science is no more a classified inventory of factual information than history a chronology of dates" [1, p. 113]. Instead, he proposes the alternative conception that "science is above all else a critical and analytical activity; the scientist is pre-eminently a man who requires evidence before he delivers an opinion, and when it comes to evidence he is hard to please" [1, p. 117]. The insistence on evidence is strongly emphasized by Popper, who says, "A scientist, whether theorist or experimenter, puts forward statements, or systems of statements, and tests them step by step. In the field of empirical sciences, more particularly, he constructs hypotheses, or systems of theories, and tests them against experience by observation and experiment" [3, p. 27].

It was over a hundred years ago when John Stuart Mill propounded his System of Logic, and his views dominated the world of science for many decades. Mill was a great advocate of induction, which he defined as "a process of inference; it proceeds from the known to the unknown", from the particular to the general. He further argued that induction is a systematic and rigorous process, and that starting with simple facts and a conviction of our senses, it allows universal statements to be made with certainty, which thereby express the truth of general theories [2].

This idea, that the principle of induction is the basis of the scientific method, and that it is instrumental in determining the truth or otherwise of scientific theories, is strongly attacked by Popper: "it is far from obvious, from a logical point of view, that we are justified in inferring universal statements from singular ones, no matter how numerous; for any conclusion drawn in this way may always turn out to be false: no matter how many instances of white swans we may have observed, this does not justify the conclusion that *all* swans are white" [3, p. 27]. His thesis is that "a subjective experience, or a feeling of conviction, can never justify a scientific statement, and that within science it can play no part but that of the subject of an empirical inquiry" [3, p. 46].

Instead, Popper argues that "every scientific statement must be testable" [3, p. 48] ; if it is not, then in Popper's view it is not science. Some may suggest, for example, that certain events are unique and unrepeatable, so that statements about them cannot be subjected to tests for the purpose of reproducing the results in question; such a situation, according to Popper, would render any statements about these events outside the realm of science, and any controversy about the unrepeatability or uniqueness of the results "cannot be decided by science; it would be a metaphysical controversy" [3, p. 46] .

The Popperian view has led to the *hypothetico-deductive* concept as a method of scientific inquiry. Medawar, who is a strong exponent of this view, is at pains to make a distinction between *having an idea* and *testing it*: the former consists of the formulation of a hypothesis, whereas the latter in-volves the subjecting of the hypothesis to a meticulous critical examination through experiment. Indeed, "experimentation *is* criticism; that is, experi-mentation in the modern sense, according to which an experiment is an act performed to test a hypothesis, not in the old Baconian sense, in which an experiment was a contrived experiment intended to enlarge our knowledge of what actually went on in nature . . . *his* experiments answer the question 'I wonder what would happen if . . .?' Baconian experimentation is not a critical activity but a kind of creative play" [1, p. 119] .

The hall-mark of the hypothetico-deductive approach is that of *conjec-tures and refutations* (which is, incidentally, a title of one of Popper's books). A conjecture represents a hypothesis or a theory expounded to explain the behaviour of a given system or the relationships between a given set of parameters and entities. If experimentation leads to results which con-tradict the hypothesis, and if the experiments are sufficiently convincing, then they constitute a refutation of the hypothesis, which may then have to be abandoned.[1]

[1] Note, however, the following comment by Whitrow: "It is instructive to speculate on what might have happened if such an [he refers to the Michelson] experiment could have been performed in the sixteenth or seventeenth century when men were debating the rival merits of the Copernican and Ptolemaic systems. The result would surely have been interpreted as a triumphant vindication of the Ptolemaic system and irrefutable falsification of the Copernican hypothesis. The moral of this historical fantasy is that it is often dangerous to believe in the absolute verification or falsification of a scientific hypothesis. All judgements of this type are made in some historical context which may be drastically modified by the changing perspective of human knowledge." (G. J. Whitrow, Inaugural Lecture, Imperial College, London, 1973.)

At the risk of an oversimplification, the process of conjecture and refutation is shown in the flow diagram in Fig. 17.1. Initial information, derived

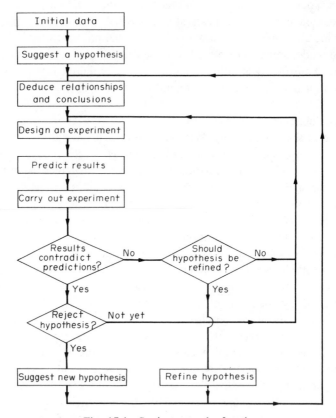

Fig. 17.1. Conjecture and refutation.

from observation and experience, leads a scientist to postulate a hypothesis that will explain given phenomena. The hypothesis allows relationships and conclusions to be deduced, so that the experimental stage may then be embarked upon. The design and the conduct of the experiment need not, of course, be carried out by the scientist who proposed the hypothesis in the first place, and more often than not it will be another scientist or group of scientists who would be engaged in the critical examination of the hypothesis in question.

It is an essential part of the experimentation process to predict the results of each experiment *before* it is conducted. The prediction is based on conclusions derived from the given hypothesis so that actual results may then be compared with those predicted. If a contradiction is established, the question arises as to whether the refutation of the hypothesis is sufficiently decisive to justify its rejection. Contradictory experimental results may reflect the particular way or environment in which experiments are carried out, while scientists lay store by repeatability of results, so as to ensure that conclusions are not arrived at prematurely. And particularly when important theories, which have stood the test of time, are involved, it is natural for scientists to regard contradictory results with caution and to postpone judgement until persuasive evidence begins to accumulate as a result of further experimentation. This is why in Fig. 17.1 the answer to the question "Reject hypothesis?" may be "Not yet", leading to the design of a new experiment.

When, however, the refutation of a hypothesis is regarded as conclusive, it must be abandoned to give way to a new hypothesis, which attempts to account for all the phenomena and results accumulated hitherto. We then have a new hypothesis, a new challenger, to serve as a target for new exercises in refutation.

Three important features should be noted in this process. The first is the *absence of absolute positive proof*. The results of an experiment do not prove that a hypothesis or a theory is true, they merely refute or fail to refute it. As long as a hypothesis is not refuted, it continues to stand and to challenge its critics. Its only validity lies in the absence of proof (by experiment) to the contrary.

The second feature emanates from the first: since the purpose of scientific experimentation is refutation, it follows that every experiment designed to test a given hypothesis should be as searching and as critical as possible. If several alternative experiments can be designed to test a theory, it is the most demanding one (within given constraints on resources) that should be embarked upon, the one that has the greatest potential to refute the theory. It is by its ability to withstand such tests that the theory gains in stature.

And the third feature of the hypothetico-deductive method is that the process is unending. The fact that a theory has not been refuted in the past does not mean that new evidence would not emerge to refute it in the

future. Admittedly, as attempts to contradict it continue to fail, as a
theory becomes more established and widely accepted, less scientists may
feel inclined to persist with fresh experiments to test it, and turn their
attention to other theories. But the principle of an unending process of
scientific inquiry, as shown in Fig. 17.1, remains; and science is full of
examples of well- and long-established theories that have had to give way
to new ones in the course of time.

THE OR PROCESS

Let me now turn to the OR method. Again, there is a risk of oversimplification, but the flow chart in Fig. 17.2 is probably a good representation
of what OR analysts attempt to adhere to. Following some initial data and
a definition of the problems he is to tackle, the analyst forms a first view of
how the system under discussion works; this view may not justify at this
stage the grand title of a "model", but it is a hypothesis none the less (and
all models are in fact hypotheses) from which the analyst may deduce a
possible solution. It is more likely than not that neither the analyst nor
the organization would feel sufficiently confident to proceed with imple-
mentations forthwith, and so efforts will be made to seek more information
(see right-hand side, Fig. 17.2). A data-collection exercise is then designed
with validation criteria specified, and these criteria need to be compatible
with or deduced from the hypothesis formulated earlier. The results of the
data-collection task allow the model to be refined, if necessary, or to be
replaced with a new one, and once again the analyst proceeds to draw
conclusions and proposals, and once again the question arises as to whether
the organization should proceed with their implementation.

The analyst may go through the data-collection loop several times, but
eventually a decision is reached to abandon the project (see STOP sign on
the right, Fig. 17.2) or to implement (see the left-hand side of the figure).
In the latter case, the analyst proceeds with the design of an implementation
programme; he needs to predict the outcome of implementation (elaborating
perhaps on his earlier proposals) and subsequently check whether the actual
results are compatible with or contradict his predictions. In the case of
contradiction he is faced with the question as to the validity of his model
and whether it should be rejected.

We can see many similarities between Figs. 17.1 and 17.2. The data-collection exercise in Fig. 17.2 may be regarded as an experiment, and its results help decide the extent to which the model remains valid. A refutation of the model implies that its conclusions cannot be implemented, and that if the analyst is to continue with his efforts, he must start with a fresh model, followed by further experimentation (data collection) to test it.

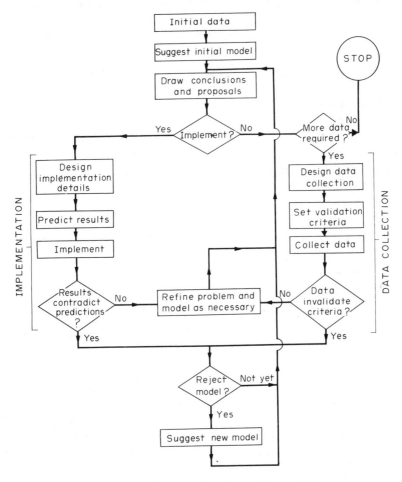

Fig. 17.2. The operational research procedure.

The implementation loop, too, is a kind of experimentation. The system to which the analyst's solution is applied undergoes a change, dictated by the details of the solution, and this change constitutes an experiment with the system. By comparing its actual behaviour with its predicted behaviour, conclusions may be drawn on the validity of the model which served as a basis for the solution and for the implementation details.

In this context, therefore, OR may be regarded as a scientific activity. The elements of formulating a hypothesis, of prediction, and of experimentation are clearly discernible in the OR process; the feedback mechanism that requires the definition of the problem, the assumptions, the model structure, and the conclusions to be continuously reviewed and adapted in the light of new information and new experience is analogous to the continuous evaluation that takes place in scientific inquiry.

There are, of course, many cases where the OR analyst prefers to hedge his bets with his predictions, either by being unspecific in stating precisely what outcomes he expects from an implemented solution, or by being sufficiently vague in recounting the possible "non-quantifiable" benefits to the system (such as "better control", "smoother administration", "sound long-term posture"). His reasons for being non-committal may be well founded: the uncertainties in the situation, coupled with limited information, set against pressures to present proposals and not to prolong the study unduly, often force the analyst to take short-cuts, and much as he would like to collect more information and to improve his model, he may be prevented from doing so. Being less than explicit about the possible outcome of implementation is both a reflection of the limitations of his model and a desire to protect himself from the consequences of the unknown. All one can say in such circumstances is when the results of the implementation exercise are eventually established, it is not possible to ascertain with a sufficient level of precision whether they do or do not conform to the predictions, and while the study may be regarded by management as a shining success, it fails to fulfil the standards required by the hypothetico-deductive method with respect to critical experimentation. Similarly, in all decisions under uncertainty, where events of the "one-off" type are considered, actual results often deviate substantially from predicted "expected" results (based on subjective probabilities). To say that the decision is still valid because one should compare the expected results not with the actual results but with their mean value (had the "one-off" reality been repeated many times) is of little help, since such a statement is not testable.

There is another aspect in which "experimentation" in OR fails to attain the rigour demanded by the hypothetico-deductive method in Fig. 17.1. We recall that the purpose of scientific experimentation is to subject a given hypothesis to the most crucial and demanding test that can be devised, since the object of the exercise is to refute theory. In a managerial context such experimentation is not tenable, since when socio-economic systems are placed in extreme critical conditions they may fail altogether; and while such experiments may be entirely successful in refuting given hypotheses, they could be catastrophic from a managerial standpoint. In the majority of cases, therefore, implementation does not constitute a crucial test of accepted beliefs, but a relatively minor experimentation exercise.

These conclusions are based on certain assumptions: the acceptance of the hypothetico-deductive procedure as a description of the scientific method, with its concept of conjecture and refutation as shown in Fig. 17.1, and the adoption of the flow chart in Fig. 17.2 as a reasonable description of the essential issues in the development of an OR project. These are assumptions that some scientists and OR practitioners will take exception to, and particularly to the various oversimplifications that are inherent in such a discussion. Nevertheless, the similarities and differences between Figs. 17.1 and 17.2 are sufficiently important, and are certainly intriguing, to give food for thought, both to those who adamantly insist that OR is in every respect a scientific activity, and to others who may prefer to regard it as an art.

REFERENCES

1. Medawar, P. B. (1967) *The Art of the Soluble*, Methuen, London.
2. Mill, J. S. (1843) *A System of Logic*, Longmans, London.
3. Popper, K. R. (1959) *The Logic of Scientific Discovery*, Hutchinson, London.

A POSTSCRIPT

Lest the foregoing conveys the impression that I accept the hypothetico-deductive method as the only model as to what scientific method is all about, I should add one or two qualifications. I have a great deal of sympathy with G. J. Whitrow who argues that refutation is not the only object of scientific experimentation, and that experiments may be conducted simply to get more information. He says (in a private communication): "My suggestion is that the essential characteristic of scientific method is the kind of questioning that it involves. Also I believe that scientific theories are not in any absolute sense verified or falsified but are accepted or rejected."

Clearly "refutation" in the hypothetico-deductive method raises some fundamental problems of definition. If an experiment yields results which are not compatible with expectations based on a given theory, should this theory be automatically regarded as having thereby been refuted? Apart from the fact that the phenomenon under investigation may be subject to stochastic elements and may therefore preclude the possibility of drawing any firm conclusions from limited experimentation, we cannot ignore the "status" of the theory in question in the scientific world (the length of time it has been recognized as a part of human knowledge, the scientific structure that it supports in having subsequent theories based on it, even the number of its adherents): in some cases a crucial single experiment will suffice to refute a theory, in others exhaustive empirical evidence will have to be gathered before refutation can be effected.

This is reflected in the flow chart in Fig. 17.1 by the question "Reject hypothesis?", to which the answer may be "Not yet", even though the experimental results contradict the prediction. The scientist is then obliged to continue with his data-collection effort, with original experimentation, and with evaluation of the results, and he may have to repeat the cycle many times before he can come to a positive conclusion. There is no indication in the flow chart as to the number of times he must face the question "Reject hypothesis?", nor as to the weight of the evidence that needs to be accumulated. There is no way in which such specifications can be made in general terms.

The point is highlighted by Whitrow's suggestion that theories are either accepted or rejected, and this may be a more poignant description of the process involved than the proposition that refutation of a theory is merely a function of the results of designed experiments and/or observations; acceptance or rejection is a manifestation of the scientist's reactions to empirical results, and these reactions may vary in time and place. To that extent the somewhat mechanistic representation of the hypothetico-deductive method in the flow chart in Fig. 17.1 is greatly improved by these interpretations of "refutation" and what it really implies.

But the argument as to whether an experimental result is significant in evaluating a given theory is surely advanced if it is related to predictions made *before* the experiment or observation takes place, *rather than after*. To explain phenomena *post factum* (as, alas, is often the case in some branches of the social sciences) merely leads to theories becoming so "flexible" in scope and in interpretation that by being able to accommodate everything they are in danger of explaining nothing. Theories then come and go at the dictates of fashion rather than as a result of systematic investigations, and in this sense the conjecture and refutation process can be said to introduce more rigorous discipline into the scientific methodological framework.

Some people may be concerned by the implication of the hypothetico-deductive method that the scientist is required to take a view, and they then proceed to argue that his investigation and the kind of questions that he poses automatically become biased and therefore unscientific. I do not regard it as disconcerting that a scientist takes a view; his position may be biased but his conduct need not be unscientific. Indeed, the notion that scientists should always be "unbiased" is pure fantasy and ignores the numerous controversies in the history of science. What marks a scientist is not his views but his conduct, the way he designs and performs experiments, the evidence he brings to bear to support his arguments, and the manner in which he examines the views and evidence of his opponents.

However, I accept that the hypothetico-deductive method is not the whole story of scientific method. It is in many ways too uncompromising, and its exponents who have fought entrenched dogmas in science have created their own dogma. Many of its adherents believe that either you follow the hypothetico-deductive method to the letter or you are no scientist. This denies the place in science for sheer Baconian curiosity; also, it makes no distinction between analytical and critical activity (including empirical work), on the one hand, and scientific discovery, on the other, and if the former is fairly amenable to a systematic description, this cannot be said about the latter.

In my discussion of the OR method I have refrained from reference to these other aspects of scientific method, first because I felt that the similarities and diferences revealed by a comparison with the hypothetico-deductive method are interesting in themselves, and secondly because most conventional OR is found to follow the methodology broadly depicted in the flow chart in Fig. 17.2. Admittedly, in the same way that the hypothetico-deductive method is not the whole of scientific method, Fig. 17.2 is not the whole of OR; arguably, some OR is less directed towards the critical analysis of existing activities and is more concerned with explorations which are more akin to scientific discovery.

INDEX